ACT

Histor.

genom Sven A. Nilsson, Sten Carlsson
och Carl Göran Andrae

115

This book falls within the framework of the research project "The Family in the Demographic and Social Transformation of Sweden after 1800". This project is supported by grants from The Bank of Sweden Tercentenary Foundation and The Swedish Council for Research in the Humanities and the Social Sciences. Within the framework of this project and the series Studia Historica Upsaliensia the following books have been published:

90. Sten Carlsson: Fröknar, mamseller, jungfrur och pigor. Ogifta kvinnor i det svenska ståndssamhället. Uppsala 1977.

93. Holger Wester: Innovationer i befolkningsrörligheten. En studie av spridningsförlopp i befolkningsrörligheten utgående från Petalax socken i Österbotten. Uppsala 1977.

100. Ingrid Eriksson and John Rogers: Rural Labor and Population Change. Social and Demographic Developments in East-central Sweden during the Nineteenth Century. Uppsala 1978.

107. Mats Rolén: Skogsbygd i omvandling. Studier kring befolkningsutveckling, omflyttning och social rörlighet i Revsunds tingslag 1820–1977. Uppsala 1979.

Ann-Sofie Kälvemark

More Children
of Better Quality?

*Aspects on Swedish Population Policy
in the 1930's*

UPPSALA 1980

Distributor

ALMQVIST & WIKSELL INTERNATIONAL

STOCKHOLM

Printed with the aid of a grant from
Humanistisk-samhällsvetenskapliga forskningsrådet

ISBN 91-554-1094-4
ISSN 0081-6531

Printed in Sweden by
Almqvist & Wiksell, Uppsala 1980

Ann-Sofie Kälvemark

More Children
of Better Quality?

*Aspects on Swedish Population Policy
in the 1930's*

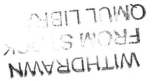

UPPSALA 1980

Distributor

ALMQVIST & WIKSELL INTERNATIONAL

STOCKHOLM

Printed with the aid of a grant from
Humanistisk-samhällsvetenskapliga forskningsrådet

© Ann-Sofie Kälvemark 1980

ISBN 91-554-1094-4
ISSN 0081-6531

Printed in Sweden by
Almqvist & Wiksell, Uppsala 1980

For Torsten, Sofia and Mathias

List of Diagrams

List of Maps

Contents

List of Tables

Abbreviations

AK   *Riksdagens andra kammare: Protokoll* (Minutes of the Lower House of the Swedish *Riksdag*)

FK   *Riksdagens första kammare: Protokoll* (Minutes of the Upper House of the Swedish *Riksdag*)

MAK   *Motion i riksdagens andra kammare* (Motion in the Lower House of the Swedish *Riksdag*)

MFK   *Motion i riksdagens första kammare* (Motion in the Upper House of the Swedish *Riksdag*)

Prop.   *Proposition* (Government bill to the Swedish *Riksdag*)

RS   *Riksdagens skrivelse* (*Riksdag* resolution)

SEHR   Scandinavian Economic History Review

SFS   *Svensk författningssamling* (The Swedish Code of Statutes)

SOS   *Sveriges officiella statistik* (The Official Statistics of Sweden)

SOU   *Sveriges offentliga utredningar* (The Swedish Government Official Reports)

Acknowledgements

The research presented in this volume has been made possible by a grant from The Ford Foundation within the framework of The Ford & Rockefeller Foundations' Program in Population Policy. An additional grant from The Swedish Council for Research in the Humanities and Social Sciences substantially facilitated the completion of the task.

Many people have assisted me in this undertaking. Margaretha Eriksson competently helped in the laborious work of collecting and processing the demographic data. The members of the Family History Group and my colleagues at the Department of History, University of Uppsala, have provided a continuous and stimulating support during the different stages of my research. Monica Blom, Tua Jensen, Kenneth Ljung and Barbro Rolén patiently offered valuable practical support.

Michael Anderson, University of Edinburgh, Sten Carlsson, University of Uppsala, Ann-Katrin Hatje, Stockholm University, Göran B. Nilsson, Karlstad and John Rogers, University of Uppsala have all substantially influenced my work. As the subject of the book covers a wide research field numerous people have provided information and criticism on specific aspects of the work, among them Ulf Cervin, University of Lund, Tamara K. Hareven, Clark University, Erland Hofsten, Stockholm University, John Knodel, Kenneth A. Lockridge and Alison McIntosh, all from the University of Michigan, Birgitta Odén, University of Lund and Louise A. Tilly, University of Michigan. I am also grateful for having had the opportunity to present and discuss my research at the Departments of History in Bergen and Oslo and at the Institute of Political Economy, Harvard University.

The staffs of the archives and libraries I have consulted have all been very helpful in locating source material and relevant literature. John Rogers and Nigel Rollison have corrected my English. Margaretha Eriksson drew the maps and figures.

Torsten, Sofia and Mathias Kälvemark have provided invaluable spiritual and practical support.

Any mistakes or misinterpretations that remain are, of course, my own responsibility.

Ann-Sofie Kälvemark

Uppsala, September 1980

Chapter 1

Problems, Definitions and Background

Introduction

In the 1930's falling birth rates caused great concern all over Europe. A general decline of the population was said to be imminent. Even the threat of extinction was considered a possibility. In most European countries the crude birth rate had fallen continuously since the end of the 19th century or earlier. It may seem a paradox that this concern for population decline coincided with a severe economic recession and widespread unemployment. Less of a paradox is its connection with contemporary political development in Europe. Concern over population was far from limited to countries such as Germany and Italy, although debate and resulting population policies received their strongest expression there.[1]

As so many times before, Europe here emerges as a unity, where political ideas and notions diffused very rapidly and with great conformity. In many countries this circumstance in itself may have contributed nearly as much as the falling birth rate to the rapid rise of interest in population.

Quantity

A major aim of population policies in the 1930's was to increase fertility, to influence people to have more children. This also means that the policies to an unusual degree attempted to influence individual behaviour in an area where values, norms and actions are surrounded by different kinds of taboos, and where change, moreover, decisively affects the lives and circumstances of individuals and families. Sexual behaviour and family patterns belong to these fields, making this policy area a very sensitive one from many points of view.

A variety of forms were used to influence individual behaviour: information and propaganda, forms of economic and other support for those who decided to have many children, and repressive measures dealing, for instance, with access to contraceptives and abortions. Even more indirect efforts were made

---

[1] The standard work on European population policies in the 1930's is Glass 1940. Cf. also Reinhard et al. 1968, pp. 488 ff.

which attempted to manipulate people into changing their demographic behaviour without their being aware of it.

Quality

Although the main impetus behind most population policies was the wish to increase the number of births, another aspect was also important: concern for the quality of population, a concern which received its most drastic form in Nazi Germany. In the Fascist countries such qualitative aims were generally linked to racist ideas and notions, but even in the democratic countries the debate on eugenics and the so-called valuable strata of the population (preferably the middle classes) was lively. Even where racist and eugenic notions were openly refuted, qualitative notions of a more general character were widespread. For example, in her report on Swedish population policy the Swedish politician Alva Myrdal wrote: "When the population fails to regenerate itself, the problem of how the human material may be preserved and improved becomes urgent."[2]

The debate and decisions on population questions in Sweden in the 1930's and 1940's have been treated most recently by Ann-Katrin Hatje in her work *Befolkningsfrågan och välfärden.*[3] The object of the present study is, however, somewhat different: an investigation of the implementation and, above all, the effects of Swedish population policy reforms in the 1930's. The pronatalist policies of the period were not only meant to affect individual norms and behaviour in a private and sensitive area of experience, but also could be of great importance for future life patterns and life conditions of the parents generally. Fundamental questions for the investigation thus concern the success and impact of policies in this specific area. Did the reforms decided upon achieve changes in family patterns? Did they affect the general fertility development? Did they result in unexpected and perhaps unwished for consequences?

Effects

Research on population policies has, to an astonishingly small degree, been concerned with their implementation and effects.[4] The reasons for this may be

[2] A. Myrdal 1941, p. 94.

[3] Hatje 1974. Other treatments of the subject are found in Iverus 1953 and Cervin 1975. Cf. also The Biography of a People, 1974, pp. 84 ff.

[4] See e.g., Reynolds 1973, p. 343: "Why there has been so little measurement of the effectiveness of antinatalist policies can be partially explained by the complexity of policies, the lack of data, the

difficulties in obtaining relevant information or, if information is available, the time and labour involved in collecting and processing the data. Furthermore, problems arise when the effects of population policies are to be isolated and distinguished from all other possible sources of influence making it difficult to evaluate the results.

On the other hand, research in this field is of utmost importance, and not only because of its comparatively neglected status. At present population policies are being undertaken vigorously and consciously all over the world, both in developing and developed countries. In the sixties the fear of overpopulation in a global perspective caused a major and lasting interest in population policies, resulting in considerable efforts to diminish fertility in developing countries. In the same decade, however, pronatalist policies were also introduced in many of the socialist countries of Eastern Europe. Recently the falling birth rates in Western Europe have caused a renewed discussion on pronatalist policies and measures of a pronatalist kind are at present being proposed in many countries, including Sweden. But knowledge on effects of such policies is generally small, particularly concerning voluntary policies as opposed to forced policies, i.e. policies which people may or may not accept.

Three Population Policy Measures

As already mentioned, an investigation of the effects of population policies meets with special difficulties. To determine the influence of propaganda and information on individuals is an almost impossible task. Safer results may be obtained by research on, for instance, economic support, aimed at certain individuals. A study of the demographic and other characteristics and behaviour of people who benefited from specific measures should provide the best possibility of determining their impact. However, as research of this kind requires a good deal of time and work, a careful choosing of both which policies to investigate and which research populations to study is necessary.

In this context, three specific measures have been chosen. The reforms in question represent three different fields of supposed effects. They were also aimed at three different periods in the life-cycle of a family. In each case it is possible to identify the individuals who benefited from the reform and to obtain further information on, above all, their family patterns.

scarcity of precise measures, the lack of theory, and perhaps, a lack of research funds and interest." — The lack of research on the effects of population policies resulted in the following question in a circular sent out in 1976 by The Ford & Rockefeller Foundations Program in Population Policy: "How can the Foundations encourage researchers to address more directly the effects of existing policies, or the expected effects of research on the basic determinants or consequences of population behaviour be assessed?"

The first of the measures, the *marriage loan,* was implemented to stimulate marriage, and especially to facilitate marriage at earlier ages and marriage between people who were expecting or already had children together. The second, *maternity relief,* was to provide assistance at childbirth to mothers in "obvious need of help". The third, *improved housing for large families,* was directed at those in difficult economic circumstances. Although this reform was proposed by the Royal Commission on Social Housing, the population policy intentions behind it were strong.

Information on the implementation and effects of the above three reforms will be used to conduct a thorough analysis of the motives and reasoning behind the decisions. Of particular interest are opinions reflected in the official political process—in this case, in the Swedish *riksdag,* within the government, and among politicians and others who influenced the decisions on and contents of the policies.

The results of this study should thus not only contribute to our knowledge of Swedish population policies in the 1930's, but should also be of relevance for policy-making and discussions on pronatalist policies in present day developed countries. The investigation also aims, at least to some extent, at providing a better understanding of the wider implications of population policies in developed countries, i.e., how they affect areas outside the immediate scope of the policies.

In this introductory chapter it will therefore be necessary to discuss at some length the nature of population policies and their relation to social policies, an important but neglected distinction in a modern context. Only after this discussion will it be possible to place the present investigation and the reforms under scrutiny in their international and historical context.

What is a Population Policy?

Population policy is a concept often used but seldom explicitly defined or explained. Different meanings seem to be implied in the concept and even when defined explicitly, ambiguities appear. It therefore becomes necessary to analyse the definitions and uses of the concept of population policy and to determine how it might be best defined for use in the present study. The examples to be discussed are, of course, not exhaustive, but rather are typical of uses of the concept in a mainly modern context. Definitions or uses referring to industrialised countries—capitalist or socialist— have been regarded as especially pertinent.

In their widest sense population policies have been defined as all state or other institutional measures which affect the population. An example of this type of definition is provided by P. Piepponen, writing on population policy measures in Finland after World War II: "Those measures ... are considered population policy or family policy even if their stated goals lie in economic, social, educational, housing, or development policy."[5] According to this view, population policy becomes a very wide area indeed, in theory encompassing most kinds of governmental policies. The opposite would then be a definition by purpose, which considerably narrows the scope of the population policy concept. J. J. Spengler here provides a definition: "The term *policy* implies intervention by the state and its agencies for purpose of changing the rate of population growth, modifying the distribution of births among elements of the population, or altering the distribution of population in space and among population centers of diverse size."[6]

But very often definitions—or more often use without explicit definition —seem to vacillate between the two opposite views exemplified by Piepponen and Spengler. B. Berelson in his introduction to the volume Population Policy in Developed Countries, discusses the relationship between a "narrow definition referring only to the policies explicitly adopted by governments for their (presumed) demographic consequences", and a more broad definition referring "also to those policies that actually do influence demographic events, or even those that are perceived to do so". On the one hand Berelson points to the risk of letting a broad definition include virtually all kinds of governmental policies, but on the other hand contends that it is difficult to draw a sharp line between the two types of definitions "and in any case it is probably not necessary to do so". For the practical purpose of the volume in question he thus places under the population policy label both "government policies that are directly intended to affect demographic events" ... "and governmental policies taken without explicit demographic intent but with nontrivial demographic consequences".[7]

There is, however, another type of definition, implied in Berelson's argumentation above, which according to my opinion might be labeled definition by *area*. Although this kind of definition is seldom found in theoretical discussions of the subject, it often is found in actual practice. Population policies are

---

[5] Piepponen 1974, p. 99. Cf. also Reynolds 1974, p. 344, Livi-Bacci 1974: 1, p. 192 and Ziolkowski 1974, pp. 446 f.

[6] Spengler 1974, p. 128. Cf. also Spengler 1956, pp. 456 f. and Kammeyer 1975, p. 375. Blake uses a similar definition, but adds a normative qualification "... intended to alter or modify existing population trends *in the interest of national survival and welfare*" (my italics). Blake 1968, pp. 381 f. — In another context Blake defines population policy as the totality of all policies affecting the reproductive pattern of a society. Blake 1971. Cf. also Blake 1975.

[7] Berelson 1974, p. 7. deVoursney seems, for instance, to use the wider concept when writing of population policies in developing countries. He contends, however, that one must examine other policies—social and economic—in order "to gauge the real interest of governmental elites". deVoursney 1973, pp. 107 f.

19

often defined as pertaining to specific areas, regardless of the aims behind them or the effects produced by them. Such areas may be health, education, military service, employment, legislation on marriage, migration, etc.[8]

For the present specific purpose of analysing the implementation and effects of Swedish population policy in the 1930's, a definition by both effect and area is inappropriate.

For the analysis of population policies, their content, implementation and effect, definition by *intention* will be used, or more clearly expressed, *state or institutional intervention intended to affect the size and/or quality of the population.*

Using this definition population policies may be classified as *quantitative* and *qualitative*. Quantitative policies clearly refer to policies affecting the size of a population, and qualitative policies to those affecting the quality of a population.[9]

The size of a population may be changed through measures intended to decrease it, increase it or maintain it at the same level. The factors through which such measures work are, of course, fertility, mortality and migration. Such measures may also affect the quality of a population in a narrow sense, namely its physical distribution and its distribution by age and sex. In the more common, wider sense, however, qualitative policies may have a large variety of contents, such as psychological, medical, racial, educational, etc.

More often than not, however, population policies refer to quantitative aspects combined with the more narrow qualitative sense of composition. Berelson, for instance, means by the "demographic events" affected by such policies "population size, rates of population change (births, deaths, and migration), the internal distribution of population, and population composition or structure".[10] Spengler gives a similar description of the content of population policy, though a less elaborate one.[11]

Whereas this quantitative and compositional element always seems to be present in and essential to the way population policies are defined or used, the qualitative aspects in a broader sense—referring to such items as "health" or "education"—may or may not be included. There often seems to be some uncertainty as to whether such measures should be included in population policies or not.[12]

---

[8] See e.g., del Campo 1974, p. 489, Valentei 1974, p. 763, Muresan & Copil 1974, p. 355. Cf. also Bergman, who, criticising the American Population Commission of 1970, wants to augment policy areas. Bergman 1973, pp. 224 f.

[9] Cf. Spengler 1956, p. 457.

[10] Berelson 1974, p. 7.

[11] Cf. above p. 19.

[12] Berelson 1974, p. 786.

Can then any policy meant to affect the quality of the population be described as a population policy? To reach a more precise definition here one has to establish the meaning of the term *population* in the context of explicit population policies.

Population is the *object* of population policies, the object that the policy aims to change in certain directions (or to keep in a certain state or condition). The reasons for wanting such change/nonchange have to do with conveniences or inconveniencies caused by the present (or expected future) state of the population. Population is thus perceived as a resource or a burden for a certain purpose, the purpose behind the policy.

Theoretically, a population may of course be seen as an end in itself; in practice this is unusual. One example would be the mercantilist concern with population which is analogous with the mercantilist wish for a perpetual increase in the riches of a country. But even when seen as a sign of national greatness and strength, population is often but a *means* of achieving this greatness (generally by conceiving of population as a resource providing, for instance, a strong military force).[13]

When population is seen as a resource/burden equivalent to other resources/burdens, peculiar implications arise. Population differs from any others resource/burden in that it consists, at the same time, of those human beings comprising the society and those implementing population policy measures to affect that society. It is theoretically possible to treat the behaviour or conditions of these human beings in the same way as other resources/burdens, but in practice the degree to which this is possible is closely connected to the ideology and power structure prevalent in any such society.[14]

It is therefore of crucial importance to establish the purpose behind a policy. To the benefit of whom or what is the policy in question intended? It is relatively easy to distinguish a population policy which is meant to benefit the power of a king, or the state, or the ruling stratum (strata) in a society. However, some population policies, especially in modern societies, are aimed at benefiting precisely the individual, whose behaviour/conditions the policies intend to change, and are thus more difficult to discern.

---

[13] Overbeek 1974. Cf. also Pressat 1970, pp. 111 ff. and Kälvemark 1976.

[14] J. J. Spengler discusses the implications of political structure for population policies and concludes: "Demographic policies have always reflected both the degree of a state's absolutism and the concerns of articulate elements in the underlying population". Spengler 1974, p. 129. Normative and ethical aspects of population policies are treated in Lyons 1973, Nash 1973, and Clinton 1973. Godwin argues that population policies often are given a form that tends to conserve the already existing social structure, and thereby also the prevalent power structure. Godwin 1973, pp. 135 f.

Population Policy and Social Policy—a Vital Distinction

Policies *directly* intended to benefit the individuals they concern should not, according to the argument here, be labeled as population policies, but rather as social policies.

This distinction may appear artificial, since so many of the population policy measures in developed countries coincide precisely with those of social policy. But then one is using the definition by effect or by area, not by intention. Definitions of social policies are numerous and vary widely but one might perhaps hazard the opinion that the stated intentions are to benefit individuals because of their personal, subjective needs of or rights to such benefits.[15]

A counter-argument may be that social policies, similar to population policies, may be used as a means of obtaining certain objectives, for example, to pacify a population or certain strata of a population and thereby prevent revolution and unrest (Bismarck's social policy would be the classical example) or to win votes and influence for, for example, a modern political party. I maintain, however, that a fundamental difference still exists. Social policy as a means to an end would in this sense be related to obtaining or keeping control over a society, whereas the population element in a population policy context is in itself *the instrument* of power through its productive, reproductive and military capacity—an instrument, which, if superfluous to stated objectives might instead be considered a burden.

The awareness of a fundamental difference between population policy and social policy is discernible in a general uneasiness in many modern treatments of the subject as to the advisability of advocating population policy measures. Whereas social policies are seen as acceptable because of their intentions of directly benefiting individuals, there seems to be doubts as to the acceptability of population policies. This is particularly noticeable during the post World War II period in West Germany (with its history of Nazi population policies). and in Italy (with its history of Fascist population policies).[16]

Although during the 1930's nearly all European countries were involved in the debate on population, today most policies which originally were undertaken for population motives are declared to be undertaken only for social motives. A typical example of this is given in the Swedish contribution to Berelson's volume on population policies in developed countries: "Only for a brief period, however, were fears of population decline the main reason for extending public support to families with children", after that there was a shift

---

[15] See e.g., Pinker 1971, pp. 3 ff., Rein 1970, pp. 3 ff.
[16] Schubnell 1974, p. 679, Livi-Bacci 1974: 1, p. 648.

"from reasons of population policy to the requirements of justice in the social welfare system."[17]

In many countries in Western Europe no population policies are thus said to exist at present.[18] Political measures pertaining to the family etc., and having presumed effects on population development, are based on social policy motives only. Opinions, however, differ on the subject. Jean Bourgeois-Pichat, for instance, holds the view that "there is in France no population policy if we mean by that a set of coordinated laws aimed at reaching some demographic goals".[19] But Jacqueline Beaujeu-Garnier in an outline of population development in France in modern times stresses the importance of conscious policy measures for the continued growth of the French population after the Second World War.[20]

Whether policies in practice are population policies or not is thus often a matter of interpretation. A policy might be both a population policy and a social policy depending on the purpose, interest and views that are taken into account. This fact, of course, leads to much of the ambiguity about population policies found in developed countries. Although there is also increasing evidence of a similar uncertainty in the underdeveloped countries, it is not as yet as clearly developed.

An example of the ambiguity found in developed countries is given in an account of Swedish population history written for the World Population Conference in 1974.[21] Population policy is there first defined by purpose, much as in the above quotation by Spengler.[22] Population policies were in the

[17] Jonsson 1974, p. 115.

[18] Livi-Bacci 1974: 2, pp. 191 ff. Examples of countries relevant in this context are West Germany (Schubnell 1974, p. 679), Belgium (Lohlé-Tart 1974, p. 193), Sweden (Jonsson 1974, p. 115), France (Bourgeois-Pichat 1974, p. 546) and Italy (Livi-Bacci 1974: 1, p. 648). At a recent hearing on current population trends in Sweden, arranged by the Social Committee of the Swedish *riksdag*, the "legitimacy" of population policies was discussed. Most, but not all, of the participating experts did not object to them in principle. It is, however, interesting that the question was brought up for discussion. — *Socialutskottets betänkande 1977/78: 32 med anledning av motioner om befolkningsfrågan.* Pronatalist policies have, however, been adopted after World War II in many of the socialist countries of Eastern Europe. Cf. Macura 1974.

[19] Bourgeois-Pichat 1974, p. 546.

[20] Beaujeu-Garnier 1969, pp. 29 ff. Quotation from p. 32. — Similarly, John Simons contends that there are at present no other population policies in Great Britain than those concerning geographical distribution of the population (Simons 1974, p. 592), whereas Elizabeth Wilson, in contrast, argues that acts of abortion and family planning in 1967 were attempts at an antinatalist population policy (Wilson 1977, p. 69). See also Hawthorn 1973 for the recent debate on overpopulation in Great Britain; Bergman 1973, and Lincoln 1975 present and comment upon antinatalist proposals by the American Population Commission of 1970.

[21] The Biography of a People 1974.

[22] *Ibid.*, p. 11.

past often pursued for purposes beyond and even against the interests of the populations in question. This circumstance leads to a value judgement: "The position in this analysis is that a quantitative population policy is defendable only as far as it furthers general welfare goals. A quantitative population policy is acceptable only when it is directed by qualitative efforts, aimed at benefiting the population in question. Thus demographic goals are interpreted only as secondary goals or as means applied in order to reach primary goals bearing upon the welfare of the population."[23] Behind this pronouncement seems to be an awareness of the problem posed by population policies in that they refer to population as a resource, as a means to an end and not as a goal in itself, a circumstance which might indeed contain implications for any democratic ideology.

According to this view, population policies should be considered as justifiable as long as they further the primary interests of the population in question. Here the *contents* of the policy come into focus, not its demographic purposes. The view that the contents of the policy may in a way justify its demographic purposes also might be contained in the many instances where social and population policies are treated as overlapping or identical—a consequence of definitions by effect or by area.[24]

But even when a legitimation of a population policy goal is achieved by social policy contents, the fact remains that such a goal may direct social policy toward certain areas or certain kinds of measures. Pronatalist policy goals may, for example, lead to a priority for the family area. The influence of population policy on social policy may be great and, therefore, should be considered for the purposes of research.

In this investigation one of the main tasks is to confront intention with effect, and the distinguishing of the population policy motive from the social policy one becomes crucial. As will become clear in the following case studies of special reforms, it is often difficult to determine with certainty whether population policy motives or social policy motives are more important. The contents of the different measures varied depending on which body, institution or authority took a stand on them and on which level and in what context this took place.

This distinction is important in any population policy context, particularly in modern developed countries. It is also of special interest, from another point of view, for the specific population policy to be analysed here. The implementation of Swedish population policy in the 1930's has been considered as the

---

[23] *Ibid.*, p. 15.
[24] Meadows 1956, p. 446, Valentei 1974, p. 763, Stefanow & Naoumov 1974, p. 149, Pavlik & Wynnyszuk 1974, p. 319.

break through of modern social policy. As in the example given above, this means that the population policy element has been omitted, subdued or equated with social policies.[25] One reason for this is the general aversion and suspiciousness toward population policies in Europe after the Second World War. Another is, in the Swedish context, the Social Democratic effort to interpret the thirties as the decade of the general breakthrough of Social Democratic social policy. The correctness of this view has, however, been questioned.[26]

European and Swedish Population Policies

To correctly interpret and evaluate Swedish population policies in the 1930's it is necessary to place them in both an historical and an international perspective. The historical background briefly traces long-term patterns of the evaluation of population and population policies, concentrating on the 19th and 20th centuries. The international context is allotted more space since it provides both some important explanations as to what occurred in Sweden and a necessary comparative perspective.

Historical Perspective

In most societies population has been regarded as a valuable resource—a provider of labour and a military force and generally as a sign of greatness for a country and its ruler. Since mortality in the form of epidemics, famines and wars has consistently threatened the growth of population and often caused considerable decline, an interest in promoting population growth is often discernible in an historical perspective.[27] Possible ways of achieving these goals are through measures affecting fertility, mortality and migration. In societies where a large population is considered desirable, one would accordingly expect social, religious or political institutions to favour population growth—most often by promoting the universality of marriage, restricting emigration, and supporting norms and customs intended to save and preserve life. The latter factor, however, has to be qualified somewhat, since not only

---

[25] Jonsson 1974, p. 115, Elmér 1975, p. 99, Holmberg 1974, p. 62, Nasenius & Ritter 1974, pp. 69 ff. For a Marxist interpretation that stresses the reproductive intentions and functions of Swedish family policy see Sjöström 1974, pp. 30 f.

[26] See e.g., Gustafsson et al. 1974, p. 115 ff.

[27] The history of population theories and population debate is treated by Hutchinson 1967. Overbeek 1974 also covers the period after 1900. Cf. also Glass 1940, pp. 86 ff., History of Population Theories 1956 and Blake 1968. For Sweden in general see The Biography of a People 1974.

25

the size but also the composition of a population often is considered important. Some members of societies are often regarded as more valuable than others; the loss of those considered less valuable may thus be tolerated or even promoted—infanticide is one drastic example of this.

During the second half of the eighteenth century the population of Europe increased rapidly with an almost unbroken trend of growth. In some countries, for instance, Great Britain, this development began particularly early. Over-population and mass poverty seemed to threaten, and a former concern over the lack of a large population was gradually reversed for fear of too numerous a population. Malthus' Essay on the Principle of Population is one of the manifestations of this development. The Malthusian fear of a situation where an exponential growth rapidly increases the numbers of people above the means of subsistence gave rise to a debate on the impact of poor relief on population growth; poor relief was considered conducive to early marriages and thus large families.[28] Restrictions on marriage were consequently discussed and in some countries legally enforced as a way of keeping fertility down.[29] No legal steps in this direction were taken in Sweden, however. The issue was discussed in the *riksdag* and local evidence shows that parish clergymen were unwilling to marry poor people.[30]

The most important legislative change was, however, the decisions to abolish restrictions on emigration which were taken gradually by most European countries during the first half of the 19th century.[31] This was facilitated by current economic and political ideas and developments. Exponents of economic liberalism saw a free flow of capital and goods as the best way of obtaining a maximal return from industrial and other enterprises; a free exchange of labour, i.e., population, was therefore also seen as a prerequisite for the highest possible economic efficiency.[32] Moreover, the doctrines of the Enlightenment stressed the rights of the individuals to decide on their own fates, and consequently also their right to decide where they wanted to live. Liberal thought, of course, ran along the same lines and actively sought to diminish government

[28] Petersen 1969, p. 421. Cf. also Checkland 1974, pp. 20 ff. Similar attitudes are found in France where an economist said that "le secours aux indigents ne leur seraient pas attribués s'ils avaient plus d'un enfant". Reinhard *et al.* 1968, p. 336.

[29] Bickel 1947, p. 153. Knodel 1974. Late marriage as a means of lowering fertility also has been discussed as an antinatalist measure for the developing countries of today. See e.g., Lestaeghe 1973.

[30] Hörsell & Nelson 1980. Cf. also Kälvemark 1978: 1.

[31] Kälvemark 1976 gives a general outline of European emigration policy. Detailed information on emigration laws are found in Fauchille 1922.

[32] Kälvemark 1976, pp. 96 f. Cf. also Lehmann 1949, pp. 20 ff.

influence to a minimum.[33] The ensuing European overseas emigration amounted to 38 millions before the First World War.[34]

During the second half of the century concern over population growth and mass poverty led to the rise of so-called neo-Malthusianism. The proponents of neo-Malthusianism actively advocated the use of birth control and spread information on contraceptive measures.[35] In spite of a great deal of official resistance the movement received a popular response. Its potential impact on European birth rates during the second half of the 19th century is still one of the main demographic issues under debate—was the decline caused by a diffusion of an innovation or was it an adjustment to a new demographic and economic situation?[36]

Also in Sweden the neo-Malthusian movement had its spokesmen. The most prominent was the economist Knut Wicksell, who caused a public scandal when in the 1880's he recommended contraceptive measures as a means of lowering fertility in order to reduce poverty and ameliorate harsh living conditions among labourers. Wicksell contended that continued population growth would be abnormal and recommended that a population decrease be achieved through governmental support of emigration.[37]

The debate flared up again in 1910, when the issue of contraception was considered in the Swedish *riksdag*. Information on contraception and access to contraceptive devices was denounced on moral and religious grounds, but a concern about population growth is clearly discernible behind these arguments. Especially the Conservatives were worried over the declining birth rate—Sweden might run the risk of losing its numerical strength. Consequently the spreading of information on contraceptives was forbidden in Sweden from 1910 up to 1938. At least among some groups in Swedish society population growth again became an object of interest.[38] In this respect Sweden reflected the current international trend.

Another expression of the changing evaluation of population was the debate on emigration in most European countries at the turn of the century.[39]

---

[33] Kälvemark 1976. Cf. also Lehmann 1949, pp. 20, 22 and Fauchille 1922, p. 829.

[34] Reinhard *et al.* 1968.

[35] Petersen 1969, pp. 487 ff. (England, USA). Reinhard *et al.* 1968, p. 350 (France). Cf. also Armengaud 1966.

[36] G. Carlsson 1966 poses the problem in a Swedish context. For the recent debate see Knodel 1977.

[37] Wicksell 1880 and 1910. A. Myrdal 1941, pp. 24 ff. Cf. also Hatje 1975, pp. 45 ff. On Wicksell generally, see Gårdlund 1956.

[38] Hatje 1975, pp. 49 f. Cf. also A. Myrdal 1941, p. 24.

[39] No general treatment of European emigration policy during this period exists. For a survey see Kälvemark 1976. Cf. also Kälvemark 1972.

Emigration earlier had been tolerated and in some cases even encouraged, but at this time, as formerly in the mercantilist period, it was seen as a threat.[40] It should also be remembered that during most of the period of free emigration soldiers and military recruits were forbidden to emigrate in many countries.[41]

A probable general cause of the growing interest in population, especially in its potential as a military force, was the changing political climate in Europe towards the turn of the century, a climate characterised by increasing tension. Furthermore the need for labour in industry grew as the birth rate declined. In Sweden a strong military interest made itself heard in the emigration debate. Also agricultural employers, who experienced the combined migration to North America and to industries and towns within the country as a threat to their supply of labour, took an active interest in the population debate.

The supporters of the agricultural and military interests together with the Liberal Party, whose leader saw, in the emigration issue, a tactical means of demanding social and educational reform, took up the emigration issue in the riksdag in 1904. As a result a committee on emigration was appointed under the leadership of the Swedish statistician Gustav Sundbärg. It produced a vast amount of population and economic statistics which are still of great value to researchers. The investigation did not recommend restricting emigration. On the contrary, Sundbärg condemned such measures and demanded reforms. An intensive propaganda against emigration was, however, conducted by the Rural Resettlement and Home Ownership Movement.[42]

With the exception of 1923, overseas emigration from Sweden after World War I was of little importance. The restrictive trends in Europe, however, continued after the war. Similar developments occurred in the United States where restrictions and demands for further restrictions gradually led to the immigration legislation of 1924. The European conferences on emigration during the 1920's provide many examples of the changing attitudes towards emigration.[43]

Already before the 1920's and 1930's Europe had thus witnessed a profound change in the attitudes towards population and population growth. Although no restrictions against emigration were adopted in Sweden, a repressive prona-

---

[40] For examples of assisted or even forced emigration, see Willcox 1931, vol. II, pp. 243 ff., Lehmann 1949, pp. 60 ff., Semmingsen 1950, pp. 53 f., Dore 1964, pp. 69 ff., Hvidt 1971, p. 35 and Johnston 1972.

[41] Kälvemark 1976, p. 102.

[42] Kälvemark 1976, pp. 106 ff. Cf. Runeby 1962 and Scott 1965 on the propaganda against emigration.

[43] See e.g., Sanger 1927, pp. 256 f., and Gregory 1928, passim.

talist policy was enforced through the legislation against contraception —whether it had any effects, however, is doubtful to say the least.[44]

International Background

In the 1920's the European and North American population debate showed two opposite characteristics. One was neo-Malthusian and concentrated on checking rapid population increases observable on a global scale. The problem of the unexampled growth in the industrialised and industrialising parts of the world during the last century was also emphasised.[45] In most European countries and in North America the neo-Malthusian movement continued its practical work by founding family planning centres and providing information and propaganda on contraception.[46] In Germany, for instance, the work carried on by proponents of the movement was relatively unimpeded by restrictive legislation.[47] Increasingly, however, the positive attitude to an expanding population that emerged around the turn of the century and received its strongest expression in the form of anti-emigration propaganda grew stronger, supported by the evidence of continuously falling birth rates. In most countries restrictive legislation on both emigration and immigration was passed. Prohibitive immigration policies, often aimed at "less desirable" nationalities,were prevalent almost everywhere—Sweden was a typical example.[48]

Some European countries, in particular France and Belgium, had longstanding traditions of pronatalist policies. But nearly all European countries during the twenties and especially the thirties witnessed activity in the field. In Germany and Italy this was clearly a consequence of the National Socialist and Fascist ideologies.[49] The fall in the birth rate was particularly spectacular in Germany which was hardest hit by the Great Depression and reached a very

[44] A. Myrdal contends that "this law against the dissemination of information about birth control, and particularly the accompanying publicity, probably did more than anything else to familiarize the public with the existence of contraceptives". A. Myrdal 1941, p. 26.

[45] Wolfe 1928 (1956). Cf. also Glass 1940, pp. 160 ff., p. 233, pp. 272 ff., pp. 320 ff. Petersen 1969, pp. 487 ff. For Great Britain see Flinn 1976.

[46] Glass 1940, pp. 44 ff., Petersen 1969, pp. 488, SOU 1944: 26, pp. 167 ff.

[47] Glass 1940, pp. 276 ff. SOU 1944: 26, p. 170.

[48] Hammar 1964 gives a good presentation and analysis of Swedish immigration policy 1900–1932. Cf. also The Biography of a People 1974, p. 95.

[49] Among the surveys for separate countries may be mentioned, Gille 1953 (Denmark), Kuusi 1964 (Finland), Ceccaldi 1957 (France), Guillebaud 1941 and Koehl 1957 (Germany)—Koehl concentrates mainly on the resettlement policies of the Third Reich—, and Bickel 1947 (Switzerland). For Great Britain see Flinn 1976, and Davin 1978.

low level in the early 1930's.[50] In accordance with their ideologies, the German and Italian regimes also pursued racist policies. As already mentioned, however, debate on eugenics and so-called racial hygiene was by no means unique to these countries. Only in Germany, however, can population policy measures be said to have consistently contained racial elements.[51]

In the 1920's pronatalist measures were thus discussed and undertaken all over Europe. A brief summary of such measures in other countries will be presented to provide a background for the Swedish policies, to place them within a larger perspective and to indicate possible sources of inspiration.

Taxation

The use of taxation, often as a combination between reductions in taxes for families on one hand, and especially heavy taxes for bachelors and childless couples on the other hand, was a frequent tool of pronatalist policy. Such measures, although often already practiced, were more generally applied in the 1930's and the population motive behind them was clearly outspoken. In the French *Code de la Famille* of 1939, which encompassed a wide range of pronatalist measures, an existing taxation policy that favoured families was further developed. Bachelors and childless couples had to pay a special "taxe de compensation familiale" based on their income.[52] Bachelor taxes also existed in Italy and from the 1920's onwards were gradually raised; the tax burdens for families underwent a corresponding reduction.[53] In Germany the National Socialist regime introduced a tax reform in 1934, where the entire tax system was reconstructed with regard to the number of persons dependent on each tax-payer; families were especially favoured.[54] Similar tax policies were pursued in other countries.[55]

The French *Code de la Famille* also contained special stipulations for inheri-

[50] Glass 1940, pp. 217 f. Glass characterises National Socialist population policy as anti-Malthusian in its conception, aiming at what a German writer on the subject called a "not unrestricted, but racially qualified growth". (Glass 1940, p. 282.) Cf. also Glass 1940, p. 458, note VId, where he gives a brief summary of National Socialist views on quantitative population policy, which ranged from a moderate to an extreme pronatalism, but always contained the racial perspective. Mussolini's views on population gradually became more and more pronatalist. He was of the opinion that the political and thus the economic and moral power of a nation was conditioned by its demographic power—"with a falling population one does not create an empire but becomes a colony". (Glass 1940, p. 220.) The birth rate in Italy never fell as much as it did in the northern and northwestern European countries.

[51] SOU 1944:26, pp. 193 ff.

[52] Glass 1940, pp. 169 ff., and 215 f. SOU 1944:26, p. 36.

[53] Glass 1940, pp. 236 ff.

[54] *Ibid.*, pp. 299 ff. SOU 1944:26, pp. 7 ff.

[55] E.g. Belgium, Yougoslavia and Finland. (SOU 1844:26, p. 8, p. 13.)

tance; the lower the number of inheriting children or grandchildren, the higher the tax to be paid at inheritance.[56] Similar measures were adopted elsewhere, for instance, in Belgium and France.[57] It must be pointed out, however, that many of the policies decided upon just before or during the war were only partially carried out. This was particularly true with regard to those countries occupied by Germany.

Allowances for Children and Families

Pronatalist policies can also be pursued by providing direct pecuniary support, as in the case of family and children's allowances. The institution of family allowances emerged in France in the second half of the 19th century where it was influenced by the Catholic church which advocated them for mainly social reasons.[58] From this period up to 1932 family allowances were almost exclusively based upon the activities of voluntary associations and/or obtained from the employers, who organised special so-called equalisation funds for this purpose.[59] An act of 1932, however, made family allowance obligatory for all public work contracts. Although gradually extended to other sectors, the system did not cover the entire French population until the enactment of the *Code de la Famille* in 1939. Along with its gradual extension an increasing emphasis on the population motive is discernible.[60] It might be worth mentioning that a special feature of the legislation was the higher rates of allowances given to unemployed mothers— a means of encouraging women to stay at home. Allowances were increased for each successive child.[61]

A fund system similar to the French system was introduced in Belgium, where it was officially made obligatory in 1930 for certain groups in the population and later extended to cover others in 1939.[62] A limited family allowance system was also introduced in Germany, Italy, Hungary, Spain and Switzerland. In Germany, support of children was given through a special "Familienlastenausgleich"; originally it applied only to workers but gradually it was extended to other categories. A proposal concerning children's allowances was put forward by a Norwegian population commission in 1937, but came to nothing. The Beveridge Report also contained a proposal for children's allowances in Britain. The allowances were to be given for all

---

[56] Glass 1940, p. 216.

[57] *Ibid.*, p. 170 and p. 301.

[58] Glass 1940, p. 103. Cf. also Petersen 1969, p. 522.

[59] Ceccaldi 1957 gives the historical background of pronatalist voluntary associations in France. Cf. also Talmy 1962.

[60] Glass 1940, pp. 108 ff., p. 120. SOU 1944: 26, pp. 44 ff. Cf. also Ceccaldi 1957.

[61] Glass 1940, p. 120.

[62] *Ibid.*, pp. 125 f.

children in a family except the first one.[63] Whether these last-mentioned allowances had pronatalist objectives is, however, uncertain.

A large-scale programme of birth-premiums was decided upon in Italy in 1939, but was probably never carried out to any great extent. Birth premiums also existed in Belgium, France, Spain and in Germany, mostly applying only to certain groups. In Germany they were given as one-time premiums to large families.[64]

As already mentioned, French family allowances contained a repressive element against mothers working outside the home. In France, the ideal of "la mère au foyer" led to decisions on special allowances to mothers staying at home in 1938 and 1939. A similar measure was adopted in Italy just before the war.[65]

Marriage Policies

Marriage and family building is considered as a way of indirectly influencing the birth rate. Marriage was encouraged mainly through two types of measures—marriage premiums and marriage loans. Marriage premiums were given in Italy and Germany but only to certain categories.[66] Marriage loans were introduced to enable people to marry and to encourage them to marry at earlier ages. The terms of the loans were favourable with no or only very low rates of interest. In Italy and Germany the loans were reduced at child-birth. In these two countries marriage loans were introduced as a general measure, but contained special racist and eugenic conditions. In France, marriage loans were given to special sectors of the population, particularly in the country-side.[67]

Among other measures which were intended to favour marriage one might mention the German efforts to reduce the movement of women from the countryside to the cities in order to avoid a surplus of unmarried women in the urban areas. The rural population was generally considered to be particularly valuable, not least because of its traditionally higher fertility. Furthermore, Italy and Germany pursued policies favouring married persons for appointments in government service.[68]

---

[63] *Ibid.*, pp. 292 ff., pp. 248 ff., pp. 341 f. SOU 1944: 26, pp. 100 f. For Spain see also Vadakin 1958. For Switzerland see Bickel 1947, p. 268. On proponents for family allowances in Great Britain, see Wilson 1977, pp. 120 f.

[64] Glass 1940, p. 169, p. 172, pp. 213 f., pp. 257 f.

[65] SOU 1944: 26, p. 113.

[66] Glass 1940, p. 243, pp. 257 f.

[67] Glass 1940, pp. 287 ff., p. 255. SOU 1944: 26, pp. 122 ff. More detailed information on marriage loans will be given in Ch. 3.

[68] Glass 1940, pp. 297 ff. SOU 1944: 26, pp. 130 f.

Maternity Relief and Child Care

The measures so far treated were aimed at individual pecuniary support or relief. On a more general level population development may be affected by investment in medical and social services. Improved, cheaper or free medical care at childbirth is one such example; improved medical care for children, especially infants and small children, is another. Such policies were introduced during the 1930's to make childbirth cheaper and safer with the hope of lowering infant and child mortality. Associated measures included legislation providing time off from work after a delivery, and protection from dismissal for women giving birth to a child.

In the area of mother and child care, voluntary or semi-official organisations played a considerable role in most countries. Maternity insurance, often coupled to or deriving from private or public health or social insurance, was common in many countries. The role of poor relief in providing for parents and children in need was also sometimes partly replaced by special institutions for maternity relief, financed by state funds or by the communities concerned.

In Germany, where a system of maternity and child care was particularly well-developed, women had the right to a leave of absence after childbirth; furthermore they were also prohibited from working for a specified period after childbirth. Similar legislation was enacted in a number of other countries, for example, Switzerland, Spain, Belgium, Denmark, England, Finland, France, Italy and the Soviet Union. Legal protection against dismissal from employment after childbirth was also provided in many countries, for instance, Germany and France.[69] In Germany breast-feeding mothers were granted leave from work or favourable conditions when working; breast-feeding mothers could also be rewarded with special grants.[70] Help from a midwife at delivery was free in Germany, as was medical care when needed. Free delivery was the rule in the Soviet Union, whereas in most other countries different types of maternity insurance were supplied.[71]

Special maternity relief in cash or in kind was provided in Finland. Elsewhere this type of help was part of the general system of poor relief or welfare.[72]

Health care for mothers and children was often carried out by private associations. The semi-official German association "Hilfswerk Mutter und Kind" sponsored mother and child care centres in Germany. A similar organization existed in Italy—"opera nazionale per la protezione della maternitá e

---

[69] SOU 1944:26, pp. 132 f. Cf. also Glass 1940, p. 243.
[70] SOU 1944:26, p. 134.
[71] *Ibid.*, pp. 135 ff. Cf. Glass 1940, pp. 243 f.
[72] SOU 1944:26, p. 137.

dell'infanza". Private associations also played an important role in, for instance, Norway and Finland. Denmark on the other hand provided a special consultation service on a public basis for mothers and children in need of advice.[73] A contemporary Swedish survey considered Britain as something of a model country in this field, providing antenatal and postnatal centres together with nursery schools and, to some extent, day care centres.[74]

The situation of unmarried mothers and their children in most countries received special consideration. This was limited, however, to legal help in establishing the identity of the father of the child and guaranteeing that he fulfilled his economic responsibility towards the child.[75]

Population motives are often particularly difficult to distinguish from motives of a general social nature in this area. It is, however, clear that population and pronatalist motives played different roles in different countries. Whereas, for example, their influence seems to have been rather weak in Great Britain, they were strong in Germany. The appearance of special maternity insurance and maternity relief also may be considered as a sign of the growing influence of population motives.

Repressive Pronatalist Policies: Birth Control and Abortion

Pronatalist measures operating through taxation, family and children's allowances, marriage loans and premiums, maternity relief, better conditions at delivery, and better care for small children may all be regarded as primarily inducive policies. They were intended to encourage people to have more children by removing disadvantages and/or providing advantages. Some measures, however, such as bachelor taxes or incentives for women staying at home contained elements of a repressive nature.[76]

Repressive policies, openly meant to force people to have children, were, moreover, also generally applied. Such measures were typically concerned with birth control and abortion, areas traditionally subjected to strong moral and religious attitudes. Though they may originally have been influenced by population motives, these motives often are no longer discernible. In the

---

[73] *Ibid.*, pp. 150 ff. Cf. Glass 1940, pp. 242 f.

[74] SOU 1944: 26, pp. 158 f. The creation of centres in Great Britain for antenatal and postnatal care—almost entirely the work of voluntary associations—was undertaken at the turn of the century, when a falling birth rate and a persistently high infant mortality rate caused alarm. (Davin 1978.) Elizabeth Wilson points out that the rapid development of day care centres in England during the war decreased afterwards. (Wilson 1977, p. 154.)

[75] SOU 1944: 26, pp. 160 ff.

[76] Lipsitz 1977 argues that nearly all population policies contain coercive elements. The distinction between repressive and positive policies is, however, maintained here with the element of *choice* of the individual as the main criterium. (Lipsitz 1977.)

34

present context, however, the main objective will be to distinguish the influence from the direct population motives in the 1930's.

Birth Control

Although the political struggle over birth control had, as mentioned above, in some countries been going on for about a century, it was by no means universally settled in the 1930's. Restrictions on contraception were hardest in France, Belgium and Italy, where the sale of contraceptives could lead to imprisonment. This type of legislation seems to have been most effectively enforced in Italy. In the United States, Britain, Denmark and Norway the legal restrictions which existed were mostly obsolete. In Britain there were, however, no restrictions on birth control propaganda.[77]

German laws concerning information on the use of contraception were relatively liberal. No new legislation was enacted after the National Socialist seizure of power, but a violent government-promoted drive against family limitation was initiated. In 1933 all associations of a neo-Malthusian character were dissolved. Former birth control clinics and consultation centres were converted into bureaus for "positive racial hygiene".[78]

In 1939 the United States and England had the largest number of birth control clinics. There were considerably fewer in other countries having obsolete or lacking restrictions. In Norway, for instance, there were only twelve such clinics at this time.[79]

It is, however, very difficult to ascertain whether or not pronatalist debate and policies slowed down the development of what otherwise might have been an earlier general acceptance of birth control in such countries.

In all countries legal abortion was only permitted for medical, eugenic or so-called ethical (pregnancy in connection with rape or incest) reasons. Social determinants for abortions had been used in the Soviet Union, but were replaced by a more restrictive law in 1936. Punishments for illegal abortions were most severe in France, Belgium and Italy. As in the case of birth control, the National Socialist regime in Germany did not change legislation on abortion but enforced the existing law much more rigorously. A new law on eugenic determinants for abortion was introduced in Germany in 1935.[80] Traditionally, motives behind restrictive legislation on abortion are moral, religious and medical. Pronatalist motives, however, were also strong during the period in question. Again, as in the case of birth control, the influence of

---

[77] Glass 1940, pp. 159 ff., pp. 231 ff., p. 319, pp. 323 ff. SOU 1944: 26, pp. 167 ff.
[78] Glass 1940, pp. 283 f. SOU 1944: 26, p. 170.
[79] Glass 1940, p. 319, pp. 321 ff. SOU 1944: 26, pp. 174 ff.
[80] Glass 1940, pp. 157 ff., pp. 216 f., pp. 234 f., pp. 283 ff., pp. 322 ff. SOU 1944: 26, pp. 188 ff.

the pronatalist motive differed from country to country—in Germany it was obviously very strong. It seems very likely that pronatalist motives in many cases delayed the development of changes towards a more liberal legislation.

Pronatalist Policies and the Position of Women

European pronatalist debate and policies in the 1930's resulted in a strong focus on and interest in the family. One consequence of this was that the woman's role was considered in a family perspective, where her functions as mother and caretaker of the family were stressed. Such views not only were given a prominent place in the debate, but also directly led to repressive legislation and measures against married women being employed outside the home. The discussions and measures concerning birth control and abortion often led to similar repressive results. An important secondary effect of the pronatalist policies of the 1930's may thus have been a slowing-down of the ongoing change towards an increasing emancipation of women. Most flagrant in this respect were the German policies—to the examples mentioned above may be added that working women had to leave their employment if they received a marriage loan. This rule was in force from 1933 to the end of 1937, when a shortage of labour helped to bring about its repeal.[81] Italian and French policies were similar—married women were considered primarily as mothers who should stay at home and care for their children.

Racial Pronatalist Policy

Only in Germany did the eugenic and racial elements, so prominent in the debate almost everywhere, lead to a consistently racial pronatalist policy. According to National Socialist ideology, population growth should not be unqualified; "less desirable" persons were thus systematically excluded from population policy benefits. A special "Gesundheitsamt"—health bureau—had the task of deciding on medical or genetic grounds whether or not people applying for marriage loans were suitable as parents. This examination in some places led to a high number of refusals—the proportion varied from 0.5 to 21 per cent of all applications. Children's allowances were not to be given to "racially suspect" families. In a proposal which was not acted upon a German demographer suggested that the population be divided into three groups—superior, non-superior and inferior—on the basis of so-called "Gesundheit-spässe" or health certificates.[82]

[81] Glass 1940, pp. 287 f.
[82] SOU 1944:26, pp. 194 ff. Cf. Glass 1940, p. 282.

Concluding Remarks

Germany, France and Italy emerged as those countries with especially well-developed pronatalist policies. In France such policies had a long-standing tradition. The German and Italian interest, however, was more recent and associated with the Fascist and National Socialist ideologies. Although debate on population could be intense in many countries, and even if at times population commissions could be appointed, the result was not necessarily the implementation of pronatalist policies.[83]

Pronatalist policy in a European perspective during the 1930's thus varied widely as to the extent to which policies were implemented. Although they aimed at the same goal of population increase, the contents of the policies differed. Variations here were, to a considerable degree, due to the different traditional, ideological and political structures prevalent in each of the countries in question.

What was Sweden's position? The answer to this question will be considered in the following chapter where the debate and above all the decisions on Swedish population policy in the 1930's will be presented against the background of Swedish demographic development.

---

[83] Population commissions were appointed in Denmark, Norway and in Great Britain (1944). See Glass 1940, pp. 317f., p. 339 on Denmark. On Great Britain see: United Kingdom. Royal Commussuib ib Population. Report. London 1949. Cf. also Flinn 1976.

Chapter 2

Sweden in the 1930's: Population Development, Population Debate and Policy Implications

What were the main characteristics of Swedish population development and, in particular, fertility patterns up to and including the 1930's? To what extent and in what way were they reflected in the debate on and decisions concerning population policy? And finally, what policy impact could be expected with regard to pertinent theories on fertility and given the specific characteristics of Sweden in the 1930's—political, economic and social?

These are the main questions to be answered in this chapter. The problem of population versus social policy will also be considered, particularly in the context of an analysis of Alva and Gunnar Myrdal's writings on the subject.

Swedish Demographic Patterns in the 1930's

Falling birth rates were the immediate, obvious cause of the fervid European interest in population in the 1930's. In many countries, among them Sweden, the net reproduction rate fell far below unity and a rapid population decline was prophesied.

Sweden stands out as the country with the lowest birth rate (Table 1). The Swedish net reproduction rate was also among the lowest in Europe.

What kind of population patterns, especially with regard to fertility and nuptiality, were prevalent in the situation the policy-makers intended to affect? Were, furthermore, such patterns homogeneous and uniform all over the country, or were there differences? If there were differences were they attributable to social, economic and cultural factors and conditions?

First, an overall outline of Swedish population history will be briefly presented. Diagram 1 gives the essential factors in Swedish population development from the beginning of national statistics in 1750 up to 1967. The continuous growth of the population becomes especially accentuated after 1810, when a decisive fall in mortality (the first stage of the demographic transition) occurs. Some sixty years later a corresponding fall in the crude birth rate sets in

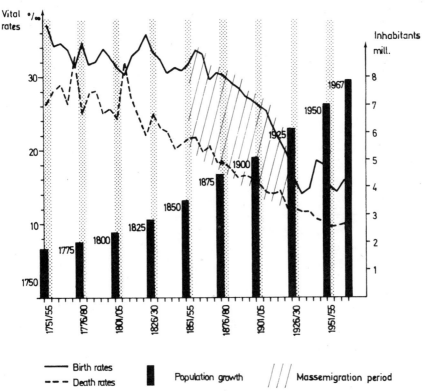

Diagram 1. Crude rates of birth and death and total population growth. Sweden 1750–1967.
Source: Historisk statistik för Sverige. Del 1. Befolkning 1720–1967, pp. 48, 87.

Table 1. *Crude birth rates for various European countries 1899–1937*

	1899/01	1909/11	1919/21	1929/31	1931/35	1936	1937
Belgium	29.1	23.4	20.2	18.4	16.8	15.2	15.3
Denmark	29.8	27.5	24.0	18.4	17.7	17.8	18.0
Germany	35.4	29.8	23.7	17.2	16.6	19.0	18.8
England and Wales	28.7	24.2	22.6	16.1	15.0	14.8	14.9
Finland	32.4	29.9	23.1	22.3	19.5	19.1	19.9
France	21.7	19.3	18.4	17.7	16.5	15.0	14.7
Italy	33.1	32.5	27.8	25.7	23.8	22.4	22.9
Holland	32.1	28.7	26.7	22.7	21.1	20.2	19.8
Norway	29.8	26.3	24.3	17.0	15.2	14.6	15.1
Switzerland	28.9	24.9	20.1	17.0	16.4	15.6	14.9
Sweden	26.8	24.7	21.6	15.2	14.1	14.2	14.4

Source: Bickel 1947.

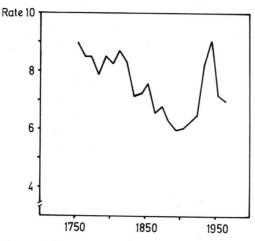

Diagram 2. Crude marriage rates for decades. Sweden 1751–1970 (per 1 000 mean population).
Source: E. Hofsten – H. Lundström, *Swedish Population History. Main Trends from 1750 to 1970*, p. 33.

reaching its lowest level in the middle of the 1930's and completing the demographic transition.

Diagram 2 provides similar information on the crude marriage rate, where a decrease begins from about the second decade of the 19th century and reaches its lowest level in 1900, after which a rapid rise sets in up to the middle of the 1940's.

Crude rates only provide information of the relation between the demographic events and the total population, but are insufficient for more subtle purposes of interpreting changing fertility and nuptiality patterns. Table 2 therefore gives information of marital age-specific fertility rates between 1751 to 1970, that is the number of children born (or confinements) in relation to the number of married women in each specific age-group. The decisive fall in fertility here emerges as from 1880 and onwards—the quinquennium 1866–70 is atypical because of the severe demographic crisis in 1868 and 1869 due to extremely bad harvests.

Secular trends in demographic events may, however, be disrupted by short-term influences from, for example, business cycles. The relationship between these two phenomena in the explanations of the low birth rate in the 1930's will not be discussed here, but the reader should bear in mind that both played central roles in the contemporary discussion about low fertility in Sweden.

The main concern in the 1930's was, however, replacement rates—would the living generations be fully replaced by their children or would the low birth rates result in a decline in the population?[1]

[1] A. Myrdal 1941, p. 8. Cf. also below pp. 52 ff.

Table 2. *Age-specific marital fertility rates in Sweden 1751–1970. Legitimate live births (up to 1955 confinements) per 1 000 married women.*

Years	Age of mother							Total 15–44
	15–19	20–24	25–29	30–34	35–39	40–44	45–49	
1751/55	–	483	416	353	245	134	31	319.3
56/60	–	451	387	325	226	122	31	292.7
61/65	–	446	386	333	230	124	31	292.2
66/70	–	440	376	334	233	123	31	290.3
71/75	–	445	345	302	219	118	29	273.0
76/80	–	454	372	333	239	135	35	299.2
81/85	–	448	357	298	215	113	28	275.3
86/90	–	469	367	313	212	118	28	277.6
91/95	–	479	404	341	226	123	29	293.0
96/00	–	459	389	332	231	117	28	286.4
1801/05	–	466	379	314	226	120	26	280.8
06/10	–	445	369	300	214	115	27	271.3
11/15	–	459	377	318	232	121	26	287.6
16/20	–	458	379	319	237	132	26	290.1
21/25	–	472	395	335	251	140	28	304.5
26/30	–	449	373	315	238	134	26	287.0
31/35	–	448	370	312	239	136	24	283.1
36/40	–	448	366	307	235	130	24	277.3
41/45	–	459	375	318	245	138	23	289.8
46/50	–	455	366	315	245	135	23	287.4
51/55	–	457	373	320	247	141	22	290.1⊦
56/60	–	483	383	334	268	154	27	302.2
61/65	–	469	386	333	266	163	26	300.7
66/70	–	445	365	308	250	142	24	278.2
71/75	–	482	389	333	265	158	24	300.0
76/80	–	468	390	333	267	153	26	301.9
81/85	–	447	376	325	258	150	23	294.5
86/90	–	447	372	318	253	142	22	289.3
91/95	–	456	365	307	243	136	20	278.8
96/00	–	467	369	297	234	129	17	273.4
1901/05	610	456	359	286	218	118	16	259.8
06/10	629	450	341	270	205	107	14	250.4
11/15	594	404	299	232	178	94	11	223.1
16/20	596	392	277	209	154	80	10	200.7
21/25	602	354	242	178	130	66	8	173.8
26/30	575	309	199	140	98	48	6	138.0
31/35	531	273	173	120	77	35	4	116.8
36/40	518	261	170	118	73	30	3	114.6
41/45	550	288	198	140	86	31	3	134.8
46/50	555	281	186	125	75	28	2	124.5
51/55	543	268	167	102	56	19	2	104.4
56/60	524	267	172	99	48	15	1	101.2
61/65	523	275	183	99	44	12	1	107.2
66/70	440	243	170	87	36	8	1	102.9

Source: Hofsten-Lundström 1976, p. 30.

Table 3. *Generation gross, net, and actual replacement rates by cohort 1870/71–1924/25*[2]

| Year of birth | Replacement rates | | |
	Gross	Net	Actual
1870/71	1 795	1 239	991
74/75	1 727	1 239	947
78/79	1 619	1 129	945
82/83	1 480	1 053	904
86/87	1 329	973	851
90/91	1 222	900	830
94/95	1 089	829	786
98/99	960	729	706
1902/03	883	708	682
06/07	892	733	719
10/11	910	762	761
14/15	971	823	835
18/19	968	848	868
19/20	1 043	922	940
20/21	976	868	887
21/22	1 007	899	930
22/23	983	882	922
23/24	1 002	903	952
24/25	993	899	

Source: Bernhardt 1971, pp. 12 f.

Table 3 presents the gross and net reproduction rates, together with the *actual replacement rate* (which measures the actual number of children born to each cohort of women, divided by the size of the cohort) for Sweden from 1870 to 1925.[3]

The actual replacement rate is lower than the other rates up to 1910/11;

[2] The reason for relating each cohort to two years is that the age of the mother and not her year of birth is given. Births to women of a given age in a given calendar year actually cover two years, if birth cohorts are considered. Bernhardt 1971, p. 9.

[3] The *gross reproduction* (or replacement) *rate* predicting how many daughters on the average each woman of a generation would have during her childbearing period, indicates the possibility of a generation replacing itself. This rate is based on the number of women born in a certain year or during a certain period. However, some of them will die before passing through their entire childbearing period. To correct for this, the gross reproduction rate can be reduced—for each age—by the proportion that would not survive on the basis of current age-specific death rates. The resulting rate, which is lower than the gross reproduction rate, is called the *net reproduction rate*. The difference between the two rates is, of course, dependent on female mortality. Cf. Petersen 1969, pp. 82 f.

Table 4. *Per cent ever-married at age 50 and mean age at first marriage for birth cohorts of Swedish women, 1870/71–1917/18*

Cohort	Per cent ever-married at age 50	Mean age at first marriage
1870/71	76.8	27.1
74/75	76.2	27.0
78/79	75.8	26.9
86/87	75.9	26.9
90/91	77.2	26.9
94/95	78.5	27.0
98/99	78.1	27.2
1902/03	80.1	27.4
06/07	84.8	27.2
10/11	86.9	26.7
14/15	89.9	26.0
15/16	89.0	25.7
16/17	91.4	25.6
17/18	91.2	25.2

Source: Bernhardt 1971, p. 19.

afterwards it is higher. This was due to the effects of emigration and immigration. As long as the original birth cohorts were decimated by emigration as well as by mortality, the replacement rates were, of course, diminished. But when immigration became larger than emigration, the size of the cohorts increased accounting for the higher rates for later generations, i.e., those who began their childbearing periods around 1930.[4]

The Swedish replacement rate thus fell far below unity and the decrease was especially rapid from the turn of the century to the middle of the 1930's. This development is even more dramatically illustrated when compared with the percentage of married women per age-cohort.

In her book on Swedish fertility, the demographer Eva Bernhardt sums up the development from 1870 onwards as "the transition from late and far from universal marriage combined with relatively high marital fertility to relatively early and almost universal marriage combined with highly controlled fertility".[5] (Cf. Table 4.)

[4] Bernhardt also discusses the influence of mortality on reproduction rates. As long as this is declining—as was the case in Sweden during the actual period—the net reproduction rates will understate the real extent of population replacement. Bernhardt 1971, pp. 16 f.

[5] *Ibid.*, p. 70. For a more indepth analysis of the development of female nuptiality patterns in Sweden from the 18th century up to the beginning of the 20th century, see S. Carlsson 1977.

Table 5. *Parity progression ratios for marriage cohorts 1906/10 and 1943/47, by age at marriage of wife*

Marriage cohorts	Age at marriage	a0	a1	a2	a3	a4	a5
1906/10	−20	988	957	902	851	807	775
	20–24	977	940	861	802	775	759
	25–29	951	911	827	760	726	685
1943/47	−20	983	842	622	483	490	(414)
	20–24	948	779	509	431	400	389
	25–29	903	700	420	334	352	(420)
1943/47 if	−20	99.5	88.0	69.0	56.8	60.7	53.4
1906/10 = 100	20–24	97.0	82.9	59.1	53.7	51.6	51.3
	25–29	95.0	76.8	50.8	43.9	48.5	

Source: Bernhardt 1971, p. 76.

What did these changes mean in terms of family size? Obviously an increased rate of marriage combined with a lower mean age at marriage and a fall in fertility points towards a fall in mean family size.

Bernhardt compares women marrying in the period 1906–10 to women marrying in the period of 1943–47. In the former cohort 4.71 children were born per marriage, whereas the corresponding number in the latter was only 2.25 children per marriage.[6] Did some families have a large number of children and others none, or was the decrease evenly distributed? Since Swedish population registration provides information on the order of births, this problem can be solved. In Table 5 parity progression ratios, i.e., the propensity to continue from a given parity to the next higher one, are presented. The ratios are computed by first dividing the number of marriages with one birth by the total number, then the number of marriages with two births by those with one child and so on.[7]

Table 5 shows that it is the occurrence of births of a higher order—the fourth or higher—that decreases dramatically. Smaller families thus became the rule. Another important consequence is that women ceased to have children after a relatively short period of marriage, and accordingly had most of their children in their twenties or early thirties. Earlier women often had children late in their fertile period.

The above is, however, only a description of the development of nuptiality, fertility and family patterns for the whole of the country. To obtain a more

[6] Bernhardt 1971, p. 73.
[7] *Ibid.*, p. 76.

thorough understanding of the demographic situation in Sweden the range and characteristics of variations found within this pattern must be studied. Simply put, fertility tends to vary with economic and other changes. The effects of such changes, however, are not only dependent on their intrinsic character but also on the nature of a society, in particular the sanctioned forms of marriage and family. Thus the same type of change may produce varying results in different contexts. Here I will not go into the largely unsolved problem of explaining fertility transition in Sweden. It should be kept in mind, however, that old patterns will very likely survive far longer among some social groups and in some social contexts than in others in the face of ongoing economic and social changes. It is also clear that new social patterns may be more or less acceptable to different social strata, depending to some extent on their desire or ability to identify with the social norms and values expressed by those retaining power and the leading positions in society.

In a country experiencing great economic change one would thus expect great variations within the prevalent demographic pattern. What kind of a country, then, was Sweden in the 1930's? How far had development gone towards the industrialised, urbanised Sweden of today, a typical so-called developed country?

In 1935 the total population of Sweden was 6.2 millions. 66 per cent lived in the countryside and 34 per cent in towns.[8] The countryside was, however, to a large extent industrialised. 26 per cent of the people living in the countryside thus lived in villages or some other form of population agglomeration.

The decisive start of industrialisation is generally considered to have taken place in the last decades of the 19th century. The first thirty years of the 20th century are characterised by a remarkably rapid development in this sector. Maps 1 and 2 give the increase in numbers of industrial workers from 1896 to 1930, and also show that industrialisation in Sweden largely took place in the countryside.[9] The growth of the towns and other densely populated places was, however, dramatic from the last decade of the 19th century (cf. Diagram 3).[10] This development implies considerable transfer of population from the agrarian to other sectors of the economy. During the 1930's for the first time less people made their livelihood from agriculture than from industrial occupations.[11] But also within agriculture significant changes took place. While in

[8] *Statistisk årsbok för Sverige* 1939, tab. 9.
[9] Cf. Population Movements and Industrialization 1941 and Thomas 1941. With regard to industrialisation in general in Sweden see Montgomery 1939, Gårdlund 1942 and Samuelsson 1968.
[10] *Historisk statistik för Sverige,* p. 66.
[11] *Ibid.,* tab. 23.

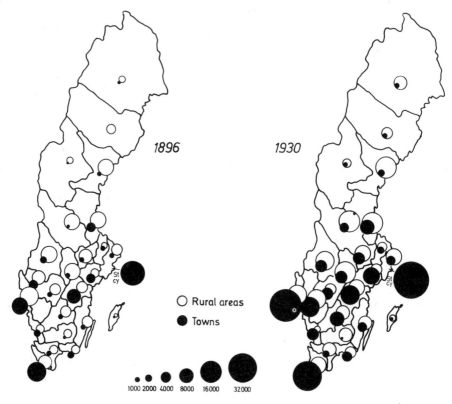

Maps 1 and 2: Industrial workers in rural areas and towns, by counties 1896 and 1930.

Source: Population Movements and Industrialization, pp. 14, 12.

some parts of the country the old type of small proprietory farming remained unchanged (indeed it often persisted long into the 20th century), in central and southern Sweden the large landed estates adopted (even before the major industrial advances) a highly rationalised, commercialised large-scale type of production.[12]

Sweden in the 1930's was thus a far from homogeneous country—it was a country which not only had experienced tremendous change but was still experiencing rapid change in a whole range of areas. It is therefore not

[12] The most recent work on agricultural change in Sweden is Isacson 1979. Cf. also Eriksson & Rogers 1978. Heckscher 1941 gives an overall picture of economic development within agriculture in Sweden. Cf. also Dovring 1953 and Samuelsson 1968. Utterström 1957 concentrates on agricultural labour. Eriksson & Rogers 1978, Löfgren 1977, Martinius 1977 and Winberg 1975 all treat different aspects of changes in the agricultural economy and their relations to population patterns and proletarianisation.

46

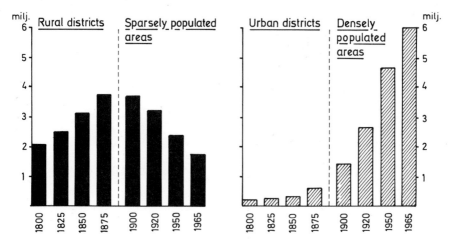

Diagram 3. Population in rural and urban districts and in sparsely and densely populated areas. Sweden 1800–1965.

Source: Historisk statistik för Sverige. Del 1. Befolkning 1720–1967, p. 67.

surprising that fertility and nuptiality patterns showed great variations. Since our knowledge of fertility and nuptiality is based on locally and regionally collected statistics, the most convenient way of presenting information on them, although from an analytical point of view seldom the most satisfactory, is by geographical area.

Fertility in Sweden during the 19th century was described by the prominent Swedish statistician Gustav Sundbärg as varying significantly from area to area. He observed three different demographic regions in Sweden. "Eastern" Sweden had low ages at marriage but also low fertility, whereas the reverse was true of "western" Sweden. The "colonisation" areas in Norrland were remarkable for an extremely high fertility.[13] How much of this roughly outlined pattern was still in existence in the 1930's?

In 1938 two statisticians, S. D. Wicksell and C.-E. Quensel, investigated the regional distribution of fertility in Sweden in 1928–33 on behalf of the Committee on Population.[14] They stated that the regional differences observed by Sundbärg were still in existence, though modified. The marital fertility rate was lowest in two *län* in the middle of Sweden, Örebro and Stockholm *län*, whereas the highest marital fertility was still to be found in the very north of the country.[15] Variations within the same *län* could, however, be great. If the

---

[13] *Emigrationsutredningen, bil.* V, pp. 4 f.

[14] Wicksell & Quensel 1938.

[15] *Ibid.*, p. 74.

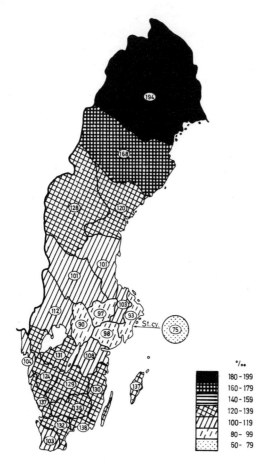

Map 3. Marital fertility 1931–40. Regional differences.

Source: E. Hofsten – H. Lundström. *Swedish Population History. Main Trends from 1750 to 1970*, Table 6.17.

average rate for the whole of the country is given the value of one hundred, the rate within, for instance, Göteborgs and Bohus *län* varied from 70 to 187. The lowest rate in the country, 48, was in the town of Örebro and the highest, 282, in the parishes of Pajala and Korpilombolo in the north of Sweden. The corresponding birth rates were 6.25 per mille and 33.67 per mille.[16]

Map 3 shows pronounced regional differences by *län* in Sweden during the decade 1931–40. The high fertility of the two northernmost *län* is especially conspicuous. The middle part of the country had the lowest rates.

During the six-year period investigated by Wicksell and Quensel, the fall in

[16] *Ibid.*

48

the birth rate was much more considerable in the countryside than in the towns. The towns, however, generally had a considerably lower fertility than the countryside.[17] This is quite in accordance with differences in fertility usually observed between rural and urban areas in developed countries.[18]

The discrepancy between rural and urban areas also reflects variation due to other socio-economic variables. The population occupied in agriculture in the 1930's had a higher fertility than the rest of the population, even if income levels are considered.[19]

There is, however, also an independent correlation between income and the number of children. People with the highest and lowest incomes tended to have the most children. There is an inverse correlation for the middle groups, so that the number of children becomes smaller as incomes rise.[20] This is part of what W. Petersen describes as the typical pattern of modern Western societies: "The better a family is able to afford children the fewer children it has."[21]

Nuptiality slowly rose during the 20th century after the great decline in the 19th century; a lowering of the age at marriage is also evident but the development up to and during the 1930's is slow. Gustav Sundbärg also pointed out regional variations in nuptiality at the turn of the century. Recently, Sten Carlsson in his study of unmarried women in Sweden up to the turn of the century has shown that nuptiality also differed considerably between social and economic strata.[22] Marriage rates were highest among daughters of landowning farmers, whereas women among the landless proletariat had low nuptiality rates and high ages at marriage. In the upper social strata of the population a considerable share of the women remained unmarried.

Although no study of similar detail exists for the period of immediate interest, some of the differences found by Carlsson seem to have persisted. But changes have also occurred. In 1930 the lowest ages at marriage for women among the total population were found among the growing number of industrial workers. However, even agricultural workers now married at younger ages.

---

[17] *Ibid.*, p. 81. Cf. also A. Myrdal 1941, pp. 48 ff.

[18] See e.g., Petersen 1969, p. 496.

[19] Sjöstrand 1938, pp. 209 f. Cf. also A. Myrdal 1941, pp. 64 f. Bernhardt has made the same observation for Swedish farming and nonfarming populations in the 1960's. Bernhardt 1971, pp. 152 f.

[20] Sjöstrand 1938, pp. 211 ff. A. Myrdal 1941, pp. 61 ff. Myrdal, however, also refers to the results of Edin & Hutchinson 1935, who in a study of Stockholm families married in 1920 to 1922, found a positive correlation between income and number of children. Myrdal suggests that a similar tendency is observable in the country as a whole in the special Swedish census of 1935–36. A. Myrdal 1941, p. 63. Cf. also Hyrenius 1946.

[21] Petersen 1969, p. 498.

[22] S. Carlsson 1977.

Women belonging to the middle classes, especially those groups with a higher education, were still oldest at marriage, but the overall differences between the social groups upon which information can be obtained from the statistics are small, on the average about two years.[23]

Regional differences are less striking than earlier; the lowest median age at marriage (24.3) is found in Västmanland *län*, the highest in the city of Stockholm (26.6). Differences between town and countryside seem, in a total perspective, to be insignificant—the median age at marriage for women in the countryside was 25.3 and for women in the towns 25.9.[24]

The main characteristics of Swedish fertility and nuptiality in the 1930's may be summed up as follows:

a. rapid fertility decline, in spite of an increasing frequency of marriage, to replacement rates far below unity.
b. considerable regional variations in fertility.
c. considerable, though decreasing, differences in fertility between town and countryside.
d. influence of socio-economic variables such as income and social status on fertility resulting, on the whole, in an inverse correlation i.e., high income —low fertility.
e. increasing nuptiality rates together with lower ages at marriage; noticeable but diminishing differences in nuptiality patterns due to social and economic variables.

To sum up—the demographic pattern that Swedish politicians wanted to influence was far from uniform. This fact should be remembered in the following discussion of the impact of Swedish population policies in the 1930's. It also provides the demographic context in which the Swedish population debate should be considered.

Swedish Population Policy in the 1930's: Debate and Decisions

Conflict between neo-Malthusians and pronatalists was a major feature of the population debate in Sweden. As mentioned above, a new law on contraception was approved by the Swedish *riksdag* in 1910; the law was a victory by conservative and religious interests over the advocates of birth control. Infor-

---

[23] *Folkräkningen* 1930, IX, pp. 13 f. and tab. 17. Quensel 1939. Cf. also A. Myrdal 1941, pp. 29 ff. Myrdal, writing in a pronatalist context, interprets the current marriage rates and ratios as alarmingly low.

[24] *Folkräkningen* 1930, IX, p. 11.

mation on and public sale of contraceptives were prohibited. But despite this repressive legislation the birth rate continued to fall. At the end of the 1920's voices in public debate warned of an imminent population decline. In 1931 the first pronatalist proposal was put forward in the Swedish *riksdag*.

When the debate began hardly any pronatalist policies existed in Sweden, apart from the law on contraception of 1910 and the 1921 law on abortion. The latter was a considerable relaxation of the previous, very severe legislation of 1864. Punishments for illegal abortions were, as in other European countries still imposed. The law, however, introduced the validity of medical reasons for abortion.[25]

No system of family or children's allowances existed in Sweden; families in need had to resort to poor relief. A fee was charged at childbirth to be paid to a midwife at a home delivery, or to the hospital if delivery took place there. Only about 10 000 Swedish children had access to a day-care centre or a kindergarten. Most were founded on private initiative.[26]

It might be mentioned that the situation of unmarried mothers and their children had been improved by a new law in 1917. Each case was treated individually and the interests of both mother and child were looked after by a specially appointed children's welfare officer.[27]

Compared to other European countries, Sweden at the beginning of the 1930's had very few policies designed positively to affect fertility by alleviating the economic and/or other burdens of families. From this point of view the debate on population started almost at zero.

In 1931 the leader of the Conservative Party together with most of his party colleagues in the Second Chamber of the *riksdag* put forward a proposal demanding a redistribution of tax burdens in favour of married couples and families. Pronatalist motives were heavily stressed both in the proposal and in the ensuing debate in the *riksdag*. The proposal was not acted upon, however.[28]

In 1934 the Conservative Party periodical *Medborgaren* (The Citizen) again took up the question and advocated measures to alleviate the economic burden of children for families. The Conservative youth organisation stressed the importance of the problem in even stronger terms. In 1934 this organisation came into conflict with its mother party and split from it. In the following election it could muster three members of the *riksdag*. The youth organisation took a more right-wing stand than the Conservatives and was clearly influenced by National Socialist policies in Germany. The small Swedish National

[25] Hatje 1974, pp. 119 ff., Liljeström 1974, p. 29, p. 31.
[26] A. Myrdal 1941, pp. 137 ff., pp. 316 f., p. 392.
[27] Hafström 1970, pp. 88 f.
[28] MAK 1931: 160. Cf. Cervin 1971, p. 13.

Socialist Party followed the signals from the south in their population programme and pleaded for a "qualified" population growth, where that part of the population which was considered racially most valuable would answer for the demographic reproduction of the country.[29]

The Agrarian Party also touched upon the population issue. Their programme particularly stressed the value of the rural population, both qualitatively and quantitatively. The rural population was considered to represent the most valuable source of demographic renewal in the country. This view had its counterpart elsewhere, in France for instance and particularly in Germany. A Swedish economist discussed it at length in a book dealing with the Swedish population problem and agriculture.[30]

Traditionally, the Conservatives, whether calling for restrictions on emigration, immigration or contraception, had been the most active advocates of population policies. Their alarm for the population development is therefore far from surprising. The leftist parties in Swedish politics had, however, maintained a hostile or at least suspicious attitude towards such policies.

The Myrdals and the Population Dilemma

In 1934, however, a new phase in the debate was introduced when two prominent Social Democrats, Alva and Gunnar Myrdal, published a book entitled *Kris i befolkningsfrågan* (Crisis in the Population Question).[31] Stressing the impending threat of population decline, the Myrdals demanded social reform as the only possible remedy for the situation. Neo-Malthusianism had played an important role in enabling the people to improve their living conditions by having fewer children. Now, however, society had to redistribute resources in order to give people the possibility of having the number of children they wanted—three per family was necessary to stop the threatening decline. But population policies should be based on the concept of "voluntary parenthood", and should not be coercive. The law on contraception of 1910 ought therefore to be abolished, abortion to be liberalised and organised information on sexual matters to be introduced. It may also be mentioned that the Myrdals saw immigration as an unrealistic alternative to solve the problem of population decline.[32]

[29] Cervin 1971, pp. 13 f. For the political ideology of the conservative youth organisation see Torstendahl 1969, pp. 62 ff.

[30] Cervin 1971, p. 14. Sommarin 1935.

[31] The book met with great interest. 16000 copies were sold which by the Swedish standards of that time, was a considerable number. (Hatje 1974, p. 8.)

[32] A. and G. Myrdal 1934. Cf. also Cervin 1971, pp. 16 ff., Hatje 1974, pp. 15 ff. and Glass 1940, pp. 316 f.

52

In their book the Myrdals also put forward a whole range of proposals for measures in the area, mainly directed at the economically least well situated parts of the population. New mothers in poor circumstances should get special economic relief. Tax deductions ought to be introduced for families with children. Housing for poor families with many children should be subsidised. Child nutrition ought to be improved by free school meals and price reductions on essential provisions. Nurseries and day-care centres had to be created in order to provide children with early stimulation and working mothers with child care. The Swedish people should, moreover, get good information and education on problems concerning housing, nutrition, education and health.[33]

All of the proposals thus had social policy content aimed at benefiting families, and especially families in the poorer strata of the population. The Myrdals on the whole succeeded in making their population policy programme acceptable to their party colleagues. At a Social Democrat party congress Gustav Möller, the Minister of Social Affairs, made the statement that he did not care about scaring the Liberal and Conservative parties with the threat of depopulation as long as it made them accept policies of social reform.[34]

How did the Myrdals conceive the relation between population policy on one hand and social policy on the other? Both in *Kris i befolkningsfrågan* and later publications they stressed the importance of quality in a population when quantity was threatened. In her book on Swedish population policy, *Nation and Family*, Alva Myrdal thus made the following statement: "When the population fails to regenerate itself, the problem of how the human material may be preserved and improved becomes urgent."[35] This position leads to a qualitative population policy with a *social* policy content—as evident from the proposals in *Kris i befolkningsfrågan*. Alva Myrdal, does not, however, see the population motive as a means for social reform as Gustav Möller did in his abovementioned statement. On the contrary, she points to the primacy of the population motive over social ones—"the population crisis must make us rethink all social objectives and programs" and "social policy had to be reconsidered in the light of the findings of demographic science".[36]

The essence of the population decline is said to be a crisis in the family—"the family crisis represents the microcosmic view of what under the macrocosmic aspect stands out as the population problem". As a consequence

[33] A. and G. Myrdal 1934.
[34] Quoted in Hatje 1974, p. 31.
[35] A. Myrdal 1941, p. 94.
[36] *Ibid.*, p. 2 and p. 9. Cf. also the following "the population problem concerns the very foundations of the social structure ... a problem of such giant dimensions calls for nothing less than complete social redirection".

"the task of our generation is to reintegrate the family in larger society".[37] This has to be done because, "influencing the whole structure of modern social life may be the only effective way of controlling the development of the family institution, including the factor of procreation".[38] A development of a complete family programme adapted to demographic planning is needed.[39]

Alva Myrdal, however, later denounced this standpoint. In 1967 she writes in the preface to a new edition of *Nation and Family:* "I should now reduce any semblance I might have to a "pronatalist" approach; the fact that population trends in Sweden during the 1920's and 1930's if *unchecked* pointed in the direction of depopulation was a temporary thing, serving to dramatize the message of our work on formulating a social family policy".[40]

Also Gunnar Myrdal maintained that social policy had to be governed by population policy motives, implying "simply an intensification of the important part of social policy which bears upon the family and children".[41] Both Alva and Gunnar Myrdal explain this view with the central economic importance of population—children are the "chief economic asset" of a nation. [42] The state has to realise the vital significance of this economic asset and accordingly invest in it—by social policy. Since population is the principal part of a nation's wealth, it is an investment that "can be even more profitable than investments in factoring and machines and other property which rust can corrupt and the moth consume".[43]

Gunnar Myrdal also expresses the view that social policy may be a practicable means "in the fight to create a positive interest in the heart of the people for the fate of the population ... Many citizens whom it would certainly be difficult to induce to adopt a positive attitude in the population question ... reveal an immediate understanding when they see that the means of achieving this policy correspond to what they have already been striving for on other grounds for decades."[44]

The Myrdals predicted that population policy would become the critical political issue for decades to come; thus it had to govern social policy and to do this from a mainly qualitative stand on population.[45] This, in turn, led to a strong emphasis on the family as a social institution.

---

[37] *Ibid.*, p. 7.
[38] *Ibid.*, p. 6.
[39] *Ibid.*, p. 10.
[40] A. Myrdal, new ed. 1967, p. XVIII.
[41] G. Myrdal 1940, p. 207.
[42] A. Myrdal 1941, p. XXII.
[43] G. Myrdal 1940, p. 207.
[44] *Ibid.*, pp. 208 f.
[45] A. Myrdal 1941, p. XXII, p. 2.

The Myrdals accounted for their position on the population question in an unusually extensive and coherent manner. Apart from their influence on the Swedish population policies of the 1930's which will be discussed below, they also have a special significance in having more than anyone else propagated their views on Swedish population policy, its main goals and most important expressions to a domestic and international audience.[46]

The publishing of *Kris i befolkningsfrågan* gave rise to an intense debate —books, pamphlets, and articles were published on the subject. The political opposition to the right greeted the Myrdals' contribution rather favourably, although their extensive social policy programme met with suspicion. From the far right the criticism was severe, however, for their refusal to introduce racial motives.[47] To the left it also encountered suspicion and criticism, but for other reasons. The Communist Party denounced pronatalist policy from a Marxist point of view, maintaining that it was only aiming at securing the reproduction of labour and military force in order to keep labour superfluous enough to keep wages down and supply soldiers in an atmosphere of military armament.[48]

Proposed and Adopted Policies

Despite the Myrdals' book it was, however, not the Social Democrats, but rather the Conservative and Liberal parties that raised the question in the *riksdag* in 1935. The Conservatives put forward two bills on the issue, the Liberals likewise two.[49] Even more active in the matter were the three *riksdag* members of the so-called *Nationella gruppen* (the National Group)—the representatives of the aforementioned former youth organisation of the Conservative Party. They introduced no less than six bills in the Second Chamber of the *riksdag*, one of them demanding the introduction of marriage loans after German fashion.[50]

In the bills and during the ensuing debate the parties generally defined the problem as concerning no less than the continued existence of the Swedish people. The right-wing press eagerly followed up the debate and underlined

---

[46] In addition to the books mentioned here, the Myrdals also published articles on the subject. They were also among the main informers of D. V. Glass when he wrote his report on European population policies. (Glass 1940, pp. 314 ff.) Cf. A. Myrdal 1939 and G. Myrdal 1938.

[47] On the debate see Cervin 1971, passim. Hatje 1974, pp. 16 ff. Racist criticism by e.g. Åkerlund 1935.

[48] Cervin 1971, pp. 92 ff. Hatje 1974, p. 16.

[49] MFK 1935: 1, 230, 231, MAK 1935: 407.

[50] MAK 1935: 3, 4, 6, 7, 8, 9.

the importance of the population problem; the liberal newspapers showed less interest.[51]

It was generally argued that the expected population decline would lead to unfavourable economic consequences and that the age structure would be distorted with too great a proportion of old people as a consequence. The Conservatives and other right-wing politicians in particular stressed that population decline would mean that Sweden's existence as a nation was threatened—immigration was not seen as a desirable solution.[52]

Roughly two alternative arguments dealing with the reasons for the decline of the birth rate are discernible. According to the first the decline in the birth rate was connected with a general rise in the standard of living, accompanied by a wish for a comfortable life and for other things instead of children. It also implied a "moral" deterioration (meaning the use of family limitation) and a diminishing feeling of responsibility for the nation and succeeding generations. According to the second view, the decline was caused by the current economic crisis. Unemployment and general economic difficulties made it impossible for families to have children. This explanation was propounded by the Social Democrats. The Liberals meant that the development was caused by a combination of these two factors—that is, an ongoing long-term decline had been aggravated by the present crisis.[53]

Many concrete proposals on policy measures were also launched: employment security for women at childbirth, improved aid at delivery and increased economic support at childbirth, support to widows and other persons unable to provide for their children, special pensions for mothers with at least four children, free meals and free books for children at school, family insurance, tax reductions, improved housing, marriage loans, and better salaries for young employees with a higher education.

The latter measure was proposed by the National Group which showed a particular concern for middle class groups and also used racist arguments. Also the Conservatives considered the middle class as a group of strategic importance for a qualitatively valuable demographic reproduction.

The rural population was considered by all three parties to be of great importance. Out-migration from the countryside ought to be prevented by support to agriculture and by better housing (an investigation of housing in the countryside had recently revealed shockingly bad conditions).[54]

Although the political opposition to the right was suspicious of the social

[51] Summaries of the debate are given in Cervin 1971, pp. 41 ff., Hatje 1974, p. 20.
[52] Cervin 1971, pp. 48 ff.
[53] Kälvemark 1977:2, pp. 112 ff.
[54] Cervin 1971, pp. 58 f. Hatje 1974, pp. 20 ff.

policy programme of the Social Democrats, many of their population policy proposals contained clear social policy elements. As the somewhat surprised Social Democrats pointed out, this meant something of a breakthrough for a new attitude in this respect within the Liberal and Conservative parties.[55]

As a result of the various bills and decisions in the *riksdag*, a Royal Committee on Population was appointed. The Minister of Social Affairs drew up a set of guiding principles for the committee. Through effective information on the population problem a sense of responsibility for the future of the nation was to be aroused among the Swedish people. Suggestions on appropriate measures to promote earlier marriages and increased fertility were to be made. Within the social policy area the main goal should be to lower the costs of having children for individual families, a goal which would also result in an improvement in the quality of the Swedish population. A large number of the proposals put forward in the *riksdag* were also mentioned in the guidelines. Politicians from the Conservative, Liberal, Agrarian and Social Democratic parties, with Gunnar Myrdal being one of the most active, were included in the committee.[56]

During the period 1935–38 the committee published no less than 18 reports. These reports contained the results of a large number of investigations as well as proposals for action in different areas. Trying to promote the idea of "voluntary parenthood", the committee proposed that information on birth control and sexual matters be given at birth clinics and maternity centres. Special courses and centres should also be created for this purpose. The law on contraceptives of 1910 ought to be done away with and all pharmacies should be obliged to stock contraceptives. The results of this far-reaching proposal were minimal; the already obsolete law against contraceptives was repealed in 1938, and a very limited economic support for the instruction of high school teachers on sexual matters was implemented.

Pronatalist motives, however, evidently influenced the new law on abortion of 1938. This law was prepared by a special committee, but the population committee when requested to comment upon it, rejected social grounds for abortion. Legislation and measures introduced in the birth control and abortion policy area thus promoted direct pronatalist goals rather than the idea of "voluntary parenthood" purposed by the Myrdals and the population committee.[57]

A main principle of the population committee was that society should pay the economic costs of childbirth. Free deliveries and free preventive mother and child care ought to be made available. The decision of the *riksdag* was

---

[55] Cf. Hatje 1974, pp. 26 ff.

[56] *Ibid.*, pp. 27 ff.

[57] Hatje 1974, pp. 32 ff., pp. 119 ff. Cf. also Liljeström 1974.

based on these principles; the implementation of the decision, however, rested with the county councils (*landsting*) which were and still are responsible for hospitals and medical care within their respective areas.[58]

The committee also proposed the introduction of general allowances to every woman at childbirth, regardless of her economic position. This proposal was, however, rejected in the *riksdag*. Another proposal on maternity relief to mothers in "special need of help" was, on the other hand, passed and constituted one of the main results of the population committee. The major responsibility for the maternity relief programme was placed on the abovementioned county councils. Maternity relief was to be given—preferably in kind—by the local child welfare boards. This reform, its background, implementation and possible effects will be treated more extensively below.

The committee also proposed a modified version of the marriage loan originally suggested by the National Group. Also in this case the committee met with success. A sum of 2 million Sw. crowns was initially granted and the handling of the loans was given to the National Bank of Sweden. The marriage loans constitute the most outspoken pronatalist reform proposed by the population committee and will also be treated extensively below.

But the major and more expensive of the committee proposals were turned down. These proposals aimed at a redistribution of income between families with and families without children. Allowances were to be given in the form of free school meals, free clothing and shoes, free medicine, and what was classified as "essential food" to those in need. These allowances were to be given out not in cash, but in kind. This, in turn, implied that a rather complicated administration would have had to be created. Only an insignificant amount of money was actually granted—some for free medicine, and even less, for free school meals.

An important achievement was, however, the passing of a new law in 1939 that provided job security for women at marriage, during pregnancy and childbirth. In this context the committee also proposed the building of day-care centres to facilitate the possibilities for mothers to work. But here nothing much happened as a result of the committee's efforts. In other respects, women's position in society may have been unfavourably influenced by the population debate and measures. As mentioned above, the new law on abortion in 1938 was no doubt influenced by pronatalist motives. The difficult position of unmarried mothers was also disregarded. The goal was to make unmarried mothers "respected" members of society, rather than to make abortion the acceptable alternative.[59]

---

[58] Hatje 1974, pp. 32 ff. Cf. also Nevéus 1972, p. 58, p. 115, and Nilsson 1966, pp. 162 f.
[59] Hatje 1974, pp. 39 f., p. 42, pp. 191 f., p. 196.

Ann-Katrin Hatje, in analysing the achievements of the committee, found that ... "no comprehensive reforms were carried out in the latter part of the thirties".[60] The areas in which the committee met with success had, moreover, generally been prepared in advance by other committees and governmental investigations.[61]

Social policy and population policy motives were mixed in the work of the Committee on Population. A majority spoke for social policy, i.e., they advocated qualitative population policy goals, but there were also spokesmen for a rather radical quantitative pronatalism.[62]

The hypothetical outcome of those policies of the committee, which were implemented will be considered in the following sections against the background of the prevailing fertility patterns in Sweden.

Population Policies and Fertility Patterns— a Theoretical Perspective

The success of pronatalist policies is naturally dependent on how well they are adapted to the specific patterns of fertility which they are intended to affect. Conversely, different fertility (and marriage) patterns will require different types of policies. To facilitate a discussion of the relationship between fertility patterns and pronatalist policies in Sweden in the 1930's, a simplified outline of the different possibilities, as they apply to the Swedish context, are presented below.

With regard to fertility, one extreme possibility is a pattern of non-planning. In reality, however, marriage plays a decisive role. Therefore such a fertility pattern will be defined as one where fertility within marriage is *not* subject to planning, control or limitation, but fertility outside marriage *is* subject to such control, as well as being considered unacceptable. The other extreme is a fertility pattern where planning, control and limitation are realised throughout. In practice, however, various degrees of consistency in planning and limitation are attainable. A pattern of consistent planning seems to have been realised in Sweden of today where access to birth control is general and abortions are free.[63]

In the 1930's, however, Sweden was experiencing rapid fertility changes. As shown above, the Swedish fertility pattern was very varied in spite of a general rapid decline in overall fertility. Childbearing outside marriage, though no

---

[60] *Ibid.*, p. 239.
[61] *Ibid.*, pp. 43 ff., 66 ff.
[62] *Ibid.*, p. 42.
[63] Swedish Legislation on Birth Control. (The Swedish Institute 1977). Sundström 1976.

longer legally punished, was not socially accepted. Marriage thus served as one important regulator of fertility. Furthermore, the transition to a fertility pattern characterised by small families and the consistent use of birth control was still going on. Some groups in the population had fewer children than others. Especially in the large cities there were few children per family and completed family size was small. In other parts of Sweden, particularly in the north, the existing high fertility rates probably indicate that consistent family limitation was not general. The same might also have been true of specific strata among the population in areas otherwise showing low fertility.

In a discussion on the impact of different types of population policies it becomes necessary to consider the determinants of fertility, particularly in the so-called developed countries. What determines desired and actual family size? Why do people limit the size of their families? What determines the extent to which birth control is used?

The connection between poverty and large families is well-known.[64] Lack of resources, a feeling of helplessness, short time horizons, poor communications between husband and wife, and usually also a difficult situation for wives, are among the determining factors. These determinants appear to be roughly applicable in Norrland, an area known for its poverty, and to the poor among the working classes both in the countryside and in the cities. An example of such behaviour is discernible among a group of agricultural workers who worked on the large estates in the middle of Sweden. These workers, paid in kind, were well-known for their poverty and for their large families. A study of these labourers has shown that while fertility fell among other rural groups, such as farmers, it remained persistently high among these workers.[65] Their family patterns point towards the absence of or only the limited use of family planning.

It seems likely that some groups in the Swedish population did not engage in family planning, and probably did not use birth control or only used it inconsistently. A regional variation, with Norrland as a high fertility area, and the large families among the rural population and among the poor in the cities support this assumption.

Although the absolute size of those not engaging in family planning or engaging in it in only a limited fashion was not large, they are important both because the expected impact of pronatalist policies might be quite different for them than for others, and because one of the reforms under investigation here, housing for large families, focuses precisely on this kind of fertility pattern.

The discussion on the determinants of fertility in advanced countries, how-

---

[64] Askham 1975, Rainwater 1960.
[65] Eriksson & Rogers 1978.

ever, concentrates mainly upon birth control, family limitation and the reasons for it. The role of access to knowledge of birth control practices and contraceptives in affecting fertility will, however, not be considered. As mentioned above, knowledge of birth control practices was probably widespread in Swedish society and though access to contraceptives may have been more limited, they were rapidly being dispersed, not least as a result of the efforts of the neo-Malthusian organisations. Unfavourable attitudes, especially religious attitudes, to birth control may have affected some strata of the population, but these strata were probably numerically insignificant.

In the vast literature on the determinants of fertility in advanced countries, the cost—benefit argument is one of the most often recurring. According to this argument the size of the family is principally determined by two factors: the cost of children and the benefit from children. In the economic oriented argument children are seen as "consumer goods" to be compared with, for instance, the buying of a car, a house or other commodities. The modern, industrialised society offers a variety of goods that may effectively compete with the wish to have children. Thus the cost of having children plays a central role.

On the other hand, since parents in a modern society no longer obtained substantial additions to the family income from the work of their children, and are no longer dependent on them to the same extent for support in old age or in the case of illness, the economic benefit is less important.[66] In pre-modern societies economic benefit is considered to have had far greater significance.

Sociological arguments run much along the same lines, but a wider concept of "cost" and "benefit" is adopted. Sociologists stress the importance of the possible conflict between demands of children and the demands of other social values.[67] In an open society, where social opportunities are numerous, the demands of the cost and care of children are presumed to have a negative influence on the social opportunities of parents (and also of children if there are too many). Social aspirations become factors of importance and "those with relatively small families can utilize for their advancement the energy and resources that otherwise would be devoted to raising additional children".[68] A particular problem within this area is created by an increase in the amount of time spent by women working outside the home in a situation where childcare facilities are insufficient and sex roles unchanged.[69]

[66] For an introduction to economic theories on fertility see Schultz 1974, Spengler 1974, Easterlin 1976, Blayo 1978.
[67] Introductions to sociological theory and research on factors influencing fertility are given in Petersen 1969, pp. 50 ff., Freedman 1970, Hawthorn 1970, Andorka 1978, Blayo 1978.
[68] Freedman 1970, p. 48.
[69] See e.g., Andorka 1978, pp. 292 ff.

According to these very briefly outlined arguments, social and economic considerations would operate towards smaller families and lower fertility in a society like Sweden in the 1930's, where knowledge and acceptance of and access to birth control practices were already widespread.

Inherent in the cost–benefit argument is the assumption that children are generally regarded as desirable, but that obstacles or competing social and economic objects influence parents so that they do not have as many children as they would like to had such competing objects or obstacles not existed. This assumption, in my opinion, excludes an alternative possibility that is of interest in this particular context. One must also consider the possibility, that a radically different type of family planning may exist, a type associated with those who already have had the children they want and those who do not want children under any circumstances.[70]

One might theoretically distinguish between two different reasons for the existence of family planning in advanced societies:

1. people are prevented from having the children they would like to have.
2. people have had the number of children they want—if they wanted any at all.

This means that, at least theoretically, we have to deal with three types of behaviour in the context of Sweden in the 1930's. The first is the more or less unplanned one, where marriage serves as the main regulator of fertility. The two others are the cases where people plan and limit their families, but where they plan and limit them for different reasons.

What could then be the expected impact of different pronatalist policies when applied to these patterns? And what would the content of the policies have to be in order for them to be effective? Last, but not least, what kind of motives govern the implementation of such policies in each different circumstance?

Let us first look at the non-planning families, where marriage serves as the only regulator of fertility. It may sound like a paradox to talk of pronatalist policies in such a context, but in a society where such policies are decided on and implemented, they may also be aimed at these families and may, furthermore, have an effect on them.

The main way to increase the fertility of people with a non-planning family pattern would be by affecting nuptiality. By promoting early marriages and thereby lengthening the fertile period of women inside marriage, the number of children born should increase. Also within a fertility pattern where birth

---

[70] At present a pattern of voluntary childlessness seems to have become more common in Sweden. Cf. Gonäs 1978. On voluntary childlessness generally see Veevers 1979, Blake 1979.

control is applied only inconsistently such a policy would have an effect. Such a policy would from an economic point of view be cheap, since it would involve only a one-time cost for public sources. The actual cost of the children would be paid by the parents.

But is such a policy compatible with the concept of voluntary parenthood, a concept developed by the Myrdals and the Committee on Population? This is doubtful, to say the least, since a policy of affecting marriage, though maybe not repressive in character, must be looked upon as a way of *manipulating* people into having children. Notwithstanding, as mentioned above, one of the most important ingredients of Swedish population policy in the 1930's was the marriage loan. In this case then, there is a conflict between the concept of voluntary parenthood and the reforms actually carried through. The point will be discussed further in the chapter on the marriage loans. It should also be remembered that the effect of measures affecting nuptiality are reversely correlated to the degree of birth control in use—the higher the use of birth control the lesser the effect on the fertility.

Policies intended to affect a population with a widespread and consistent use of family planning will have to be directly aimed at increasing childbearing. But their content may vary considerably, not least due to whether they are directed at people that are prevented from having the children they want—regardless of how strong that wish may be—or whether they are aimed at people who do not want any (more) children.

In both cases repressive policies such as prohibiting contraceptives and abortions are applicable. Such measures are, of course, not in conformance with the concept of voluntary parenthood. But as mentioned above, the abortion law of 1938 and the committee's consideration of the situation of unmarried mothers contained such elements.

Policies intended to better conditions at childbirth, to alleviate the economic and other obstacles to having children, to provide care for children, etc., would, on the other hand, be in conformance with this concept. These are policies directed at people prevented from having the children that they would like to have. The law on job security for working women in 1939 belongs to this kind of policy. The same is true of maternity relief and improved housing for large families. These are naturally policies with a social policy content.

To influence people to have more children than they want, or to influence them to have children when they would prefer to be childless would be harder to fit into the notion of voluntary parenthood. In this case the policies would have to be of the kind where children are "bought" with public money—the child will be seen almost exclusively as an economic asset for society or some part of society. No clearcut policy of this kind can, however, be said to have been included in the Swedish policy measures carried through in the 1930's.

But considerations of this kind can be found in some of the views, expressed both by official authorities and politicians, on both maternity relief and improved housing on large families.

Policy contents are ambiguous and vary depending on whose point of view is considered. These issues will be further discussed when the three policy measures concerning marriage loans, maternity relief and improved housing for large families are treated in detail in the following chapters.

Chapter 3

Earlier Marriages and More Children? Swedish Marriage Loans as a Pronatalist Measure

The introduction of marriage loans in Sweden led to great expectations. By enabling people to buy furniture and other necessities for their future homes, the loans were expected to facilitate marriage at younger ages. It was thought that lowering the age at marriage would by extending the fertile period of women within marriage, result in a higher birth rate. Since the loans would induce unmarried couples expecting a child or those who already had children to marry, an indirect effect on the birth rate was also foreseen. Once married these couples might have more children.

Sven Wicksell, one of the demographic experts of the Committee on Population, elaborated on this in a memorandum in the committee's report on marriage loans.[1] He compared marriage ratios and age at marriage in Sweden with other countries, in particular Denmark. Underlining the connection between low numbers of married people and high ages at marriage he pointed out the unfavourable influence on fertility of a comparatively low proportion of married women in fertile ages—the current situation in Sweden according to Wicksell. In Denmark, where age at marriage was lower than in Sweden, the share of married women in fertile ages was considerably higher—and so was the birth rate. Wicksell concluded that an increase of the Swedish marriage ratio to the same level as the Danish would, at the very least, increase fertility to the level necessary for maintaining the Swedish population at its present size. The marriage loans were thus, to say the least, seen as crucially important in the Swedish population policy context of the 1930's.

How were the Swedish marriage loans constructed and what conditions were attached to them? How did they compare with similar measures in other countries? How many loans were granted? Who were the borrowers? Was fertility affected in those families receiving loans? How did the actual effects of the loans compare with the general expectations of those who introduced and supported them? These are the main questions to be answered in this chapter.

[1] Wicksell 1936.

Marriage Loans as a Pronatalist Measure
in Contemporary Europe

Sweden was not the only European country in which marriage loans were introduced as a pronatalist measure. They were also instituted in France, Germany, Italy and Spain in the 1930's. The stipulations for such loans varied somewhat from country to country.

In Germany, special conditions were attached to marriage loans. The racial stock and political views of applicants were important determining factors. The loans were interest free and were partially reduced on the birth of each child. Originally the loans also were intended to alleviate unemployment. Therefore, loans were given to couples in which the woman was working only on the condition that she cease work upon marriage. Later when unemployment was no longer a problem, these stipulations were removed.[2]

In Italy, marriage loans were introduced in 1937. The applicants had to be under 26 years of age. As in Germany the loans were free of interest and reductions were made on the birth of each child.[3] Such reductions were also made in Spain.[4]

In France, marriage loans were introduced in the *Code de la Famille* of 1939. The loans were reserved for certain groups in the population, in particular those with agricultural occupations. They were to be repaid with interest, but were also partially reduced on the birth of successive children.[5]

In 1940 D. V. Glass made some tentative evaluations of the possible effects of marriage loans in different European countries. He estimated their influence in France as low, mainly because of interest on the loans, but also because they aimed only at a part of the population.[6] On the other hand, in Germany, where loans were freely granted an increase in the number of marriages occurred. Even if the actual influence can never be known, it seems likely, according to Glass, that they were of some significance for the rise of the German marriage rate.[7] Glass believed that in Italy the loans *might* have had some influence.[8]

The effect of the German loans, model for the Swedish ones, are of particular interest here. Contemporary German opinion considered marriage loans as a complete success. Several experts testified as to their decisive importance for

---

[2] Glass 1940, pp. 98 ff. SOU 1944: 26, pp. 122 ff.
[3] Glass 1940, pp. 256 f. SOU 1944: 26, pp. 122 ff.
[4] Vadakin 1958, p. 105, 116.
[5] Glass 1940, pp. 214 f., p. 445.
[6] *Ibid.*, p. 217.
[7] *Ibid.*, p. 306.
[8] *Ibid.*, p. 263.

the higher German marriage and fertility rates in the second half of the 1930's.[9] Other observers were, however, more reserved in their praise.

In 1944, a German economist in exile, Rudolf Meidner, prepared a special report on German population policy for the new Swedish Commission on Population, which was appointed in 1941. Meidner, who was generally critical towards these policies, analysed the marriage loans in depth and argued that their effects were at best uncertain and that it was still too early to evaluate their impact.[10]

According to the German demographer Frank Reinders, the possible effects of the marriage loans on marriage and fertility in Germany during the 1930's are uncertain and hard to establish.[11]

The Swedish Marriage Loans

The German influence was conspicuous behind the creation of the Swedish marriage loans. As mentioned above, the loans were proposed in a special motion to the *riksdag* submitted by the members of the right-wing National Group.[12] In their motion the three members of the National Group maintained that the economic difficulty of establishing a new household was a major obstacle for young people who wanted to marry. By removing this obstacle, the ages at marriage ought to be lowered, the fertile period of women within marriage prolonged, and fertility accordingly increased.

The suggested conditions for the loans were about the same as in Germany. Both applicants had to be Swedish citizens and had to submit a medical certificate testifying that they suffered from no genetic diseases. The loans were to be interest free, were to be reduced by 25 per cent at the birth of each successive child, and the annual re-payments were to be small.

The *riksdag* referred the proposal to the Committee on Population, where it was considered together with another measure with a similar purpose—a "planned-saving scheme".[13] This other measure aimed at inducing young people to save money by making saving on favourable conditions available and thus enable them to marry earlier.

In its report the committee saw unemployment among the working class as one of the main factors behind the marriage situation.[14] The economic crisis made it impossible for an individual to make long-term plans with the result

[9] E.g., Burgdörfer 1942, Jobst 1940, and Rahlfs 1940.
[10] Meidner 1944.
[11] Reinders 1970, pp. 83 f. Reinders 1974.
[12] MAK 1935 nr 4.
[13] Hatje 1974, pp. 36 f.
[14] SOU 1936: 14.

that marriage was, to a large extent, postponed. The same was also true of young members of the lower middle class.

Although aiming at the same effect, the two proposed measures were different. They were directed at different social groups. For those who were able to repay loans—the lower middle class/upper working-class groups—marriage loans were to be made available. But for the poorer members of the population, who would find it hard to repay a loan, the "planned-saving scheme" was proposed. The emphasis on the lower middle class/upper working-class also reflects an evaluation of these groups as particularly important from a reproductive point of view.

The planned-saving scheme for the poorer elements of the working-class was, however, turned down by the *riksdag*. With regard to marriage loans the Committee on Population proposed a version considerably different from the one proposed by the National Group. No reductions were to be made on the birth of children. A low rate of interest was to be paid, and no genetic conditions were attached to the loans. The loans were not to exceed 1 000 Sw. crowns. They were to be repaid within five years. Applicants were required to prove that they needed a loan. Furthermore, those granted a loan should be "known as steady and economically prudent" and if possible to have "shown a willingness to save".[15]

When the proposal on marriage loans was approved by the *riksdag* in 1937 the decision was accompanied by a controversy over which institution should handle the loans. The committee did not recommend the usual credit institutions, on the grounds that these could not give necessary consideration to the applicants' social situation. Instead, the committee suggested the Swedish Post Office Board. After criticism by right wing politicians, management of the loans was assigned to the National Bank of Sweden.[16] This was also acceptable to the Social Democrats who found it in their interest to give the management of the loans to a governmental credit institution rather than to banks controlled by private capital.

The National Bank of Sweden had besides its head office in Stockholm local offices in every provincial capital as well as in Norrköping and Sundsvall. The local offices were to administer the loans. In addition, the local authorities in each municipality appointed a local agent to deal with the applications for loans.[17]

The total amount of money loaned and number of loans granted during the first decade of the policy is shown in Table 6. The number of loans granted

[15] SFS 1937:809. Reductions of loans at the successive birth of children was again discussed in the Commission on Population during the 1940s, but without result. Hatje 1974, pp. 71f.

[16] Hatje 1974, p. 36.

[17] SFS 1937:810. *Bankoutskottets memorial* 1939.

Table 6. *Marriage loans granted during the period 1938–1948, by fiscal year.*

Years	Number	Amount
1/1–30/6 1938	2 729	1 858 000
1938–39	8 498	6 633 000
1939–40	7 634	6 027 000
1940–41	8 992	6 957 000
1941–42	11 335	9 172 000
1942–43	13 452	11 511 000
1943–44	13 543	13 536 000
1944–45	12 461	13 714 000
1945–46	11 618	12 949 000
1946–47	11 416	16 221 000
1947–48	10 511	16 195 000

Source: Statistics on marriage loans 1/1 1938–30/6 1948. (Mimeographed. National Bank of Sweden. Department of Marriage Loans. Stockholm.)

continued to increase up to the end of World War II, after which a small decrease occurred.

The proportion of marriages with loans of all marriages is illustrated in Table 7. The number of marriages with loans increased relative to the total

Table 7. *Marriage loans in per cent of all marriages, 1938–1948, by calendar year*

Year	All marriages	Number of marriages with loans (estimated)	In per cent of all marriages
1938	58 130	6 978	12.00
1939	61 373	8 066	13.14
1940	59 166	8 313	14.05
1941	58 102	10 163	17.49
1942	63 659	12 393	19.47
1943	62 803	13 497	21.49
1944	64 627	13 091	20.26
1945	64 280	12 129	18.87
1946	63 800	11 517	18.05
1947	59 670	10 963	18.37
1948	58 009	10 155	17.51
	673 619	117 265	17.40

Sources: Statistics on marriage loans 1/1 1938–30/6 1948. (Mimeographed, National Bank of Sweden, Department for Marriage Loans, Stockholm.)—*Historisk statistik för Sverige, Del 1. Befolkning 1720–1967*, tab. 28.

number of marriages up to 1944, at which time as many as one in five received a loan. Clearly, the effect of the marriage loans might have been considerable.

Were there regional differences in the granting of loans? The statistics compiled by the local offices only permit calculations for the first two years of the reform as subsequently statistics only provide the accumulated number of outstanding loans.[18] To be meaningful, these statistics should be presented as percentages of the total number of marriages in each region.[19] As can be seen from Map 4, there were regional differences, at least during the two years for which data are available. *Län* with a high degree of urbanisation had considerably higher proportions of loans than *län* with more pronounced agrarian structures.

This is corroborated by an official investigation in 1941 made by the Swedish Social Board on the behalf of the Commission on Population.[20] Every fifth application during 1938–41 was investigated. The available information

[18] *Bankoutskottets memorial*, 1938 and 1939. — There were also differences in the amounts granted (cf. Table A below) and the share of the borrowers which had difficulties with repayments. It was, not possible, however, to determine the total number of applications.

Table A. *Granted loans of 1 000 Sw crowns in per cent of applications for this sum*

Hallands län	89.7 %	Södermanlands län	43.8 %
Gotlands län	88.9 %	Stockholms stad	41.4 %
Uppsala län	75.9 %	Västmanlands län	38.6 %
Gävleborgs län	74.1 %	Västerbottens län	32.0%
Örebro län	72.6 %	Blekinge län	27.6 %
Skaraborgs län	70.9 %	Östergötlands län	21.9 %
Värmlands län	70.7 %	Kalmar län	21.3 %
Kronobergs län	69.6 %	Jämtlands län	20.8 %
Jönköpings län	69.0 %	Västernorrlands län	20.3 %
Kopparbergs län	62.0 %	Norrbottens län	17.3 %
Stockholms län	49.4 %	Kristianstad län	16.9 %
Göteb. and Bohus län	48.7 %		
Malmöhus län	44.0 %	All Sweden	47.2 %

Source: SOU 1943:18, p. 55.

In 1941 the Committee on Retrenchment investigated those marriage loans where difficulties with repayments occurred. Large differences among the various local offices of the National Bank were observed. Only 7.1 per cent of the outstanding loans in one district (Karlskrona) were not regularly paid, whereas in a neighbouring district failures amount to 25.8 per cent (Kristianstad). (National Archives: Committee no. 864:9. Letter and report on the marriage loans.)
[19] The local bank districts did not exactly coincide with *län*, but the differences are of minor importance.
[20] SOU 1943:18, pp. 11 f.

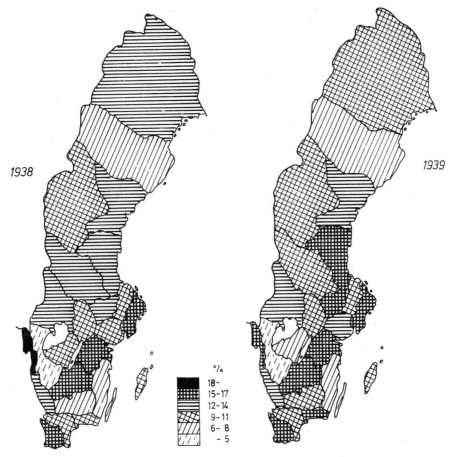

1938

1939

%
18-
15-17
12-14
9-11
6-8
-5

Map 4. Marriage loans in er cent of all marriages in 1938 and 1939. Regional differences.

Sources: Bankutskottets memorial, 1939 and 1940, p. 18. — *Sveriges Officiella Statistik, Befolkningsrörelsen,* 1938 and 1939, Table 6.

was then analysed and presented in a printed report. The report indicated that most applications were from industrial workers, especially those in the metal industry. On the other hand, only an insignificant number of applicants were employed in agriculture. The researchers concluded that the loans probably had helped to make a number of children, who otherwise would have been born out of wedlock, legitimate. They also found that the average age of the borrowers was lower than the average age at marriage in Sweden.

An inquiry was also made into the borrowers' use of the loans. The sample investigated was small, including only 164 couples, but the results were rather uniform. The investigators found them depressing. Many of the borrowers had failed to use the money for useful household purchases, spending it instead on

71

expensive and impractical furniture for the 'front parlour'—a room which very often was only used on special occasions. These families lived and slept in the kitchen.[21]

Marriage Loans and Fertility

An investigation of the effects of the marriage loans on the birth rate requires a more thorough examination of the possible influence of the loans on fertility than that given by contemporary observers. The primary means of influencing fertility was based on the assumption that marriage loans by lowering the ages at marriage and influencing couples who had or were expecting children to marry would positively affect the marriage ratio. This in turn, it was hoped, would increase the birth rate. To determine whether or not the loans actually affected ages at marriage is difficult, since couples benefiting from marriage loans should, generally, have been younger than the total marrying population, because the loans were most attractive to younger people and because the total married included more people remarrying at older ages.

Yet, even though the ages at marriage were lowered, there might still have been other complications. As marriages contracted under such circumstances might be more apt to result in divorce, therefore shortening instead of lengthening the fertile period of women within marriage, the divorce rate among people who benefited from the loans must be compared with the general divorce rate.

Even if we assume that the age at marriage was lowered and the marriage rate increased, we still must consider whether or not this affected fertility. The connection between the bride's age at marriage and the number of children born within marriage, as pointed out above, is reversely correlated to the use of birth control. The more limited the use of birth control, the greater the effect of measures affecting marriage.

Can the influence of the marriage loans on fertility be established empirically? This is possible in Sweden because the population registration system allows, without any significant loss of information, an investigation of individual families and their fertility. The best means of obtaining information on the marital behaviour and fertility of those couples who received marriage loans is to conduct a longitudinal study based on a sample of borrowers.[22] All that is

---

[21] *Ibid.*, pp. 13 ff. It might, however, be worth mentioning that another point of view is discernible in contemporary debate on the loans: that the economic burden of the loans might have had the result that couples chose to postpone having children until later, the loans then having a *negative* effect on fertility. Hatje 1974, p. 179.

[22] For the advantage of cohort analysis over other types of analysis see e.g., Taeuber 1966, Ryder 1970, Reinders 1970 and Hofsten 1975. Cf. also Langholm 1976.

required is that the names of individuals receiving loans be linked with information on these individuals in the population registers.

Since marriage loans were most common in urban and industrialised areas, the choice of such an area clearly furthers the object of the study, especially if the area in question is one where the use of marriage loans was frequent. The Stockholm area with many industrial workers and the highest number of marriage loans in the country corresponds well to these conditions. Moreover, adequate sources are available.

The Marriage Loan Cohort: Sources and Methods

Marriage loans were issued in Stockholm by a special department of the National Bank of Sweden. This department kept an alphabetical register from 1938 through 1944 of all persons receiving marriage loans within the district. Information on loans by calendar year is found in a diary. Unfortunately, however, only names are recorded. Few other documents on the loans exist, since they were regularly destroyed once the loans were repaid.

The register contains the name, occupation, year of birth, addresses, the amount of money borrowed and repayments of each borrower.[23] On payment of the final installment of a loan the name of the borrower was removed from the register. This means that the early years of the register are not suitable for this study, since the remaining information is probably not typical. The first year indicating complete agreement between the register and the diary of borrowers is 1942.[24]

Thus 1942 was the earliest year which could be used to obtain a statistically correct sample of people receiving marriage loans in the Stockholm district. Every seventh name was used to provide a sample cohort of reasonable size. The combined knowledge of name, address and year of birth permitted reliable identification of each person in the population registers.

The cohort from the marriage loan register consists of 307 couples. These were located in the population registers and each couple was followed in the registers until the end of the fertile period of the woman (45 years of age) or until the marriage was dissolved. Only three couples listed in the register of the

---

[23] The register turned out to be deficient in so far as it only contains information on borrowers with surnames beginning with the letters A to O. This means that roughly two-thirds, or 2 150 out of the original 3 166 loans in the register, are preserved. Since there is no reason to assume that any significant differences existed between people with surnames beginning with A to O and those with names beginning with the remaining letters in the alphabet, this defect is unimportant.

[24] Those who received loans in 1942 had not repaid them by 1944 when the register was replaced with another system.

National Bank could not be found in the population registers; one was lost in the process of following the cohort in the different population registers.[25]

Marriage Loans and Age at Marriage

The above mentioned investigation of 1941 by the Social Board showed that the average age at marriage was lower among couples who applied for marriage loans than among those who did not. This was also true of the Stockholm cohort, where the mean age at marriage for women was 24, the median 23.3. Women among the total marrying population married at an average age of 26.3 and median age of 25.0[26] Although there is a difference in age at marriage reliable conclusions on the effect of the loans on age at marriage are not possible since, for example, younger couples who lived at home before marriage would probably be more interested in the loans than older people who were more established.

Divorces

Is there a correlation between age at marriage and divorce? Did a lower age at marriage increase the risk for divorce and thus adversely affect fertility? The divorce rate for the cohort was high: more than every fourth marriage ended in divorce before the wife reached the age of 45. The rate for the total married population in Sweden in 1942 was 12.8 per cent after 24 years of marriage.[27] One must, however, remember that large regional differences existed; the towns and especially Stockholm had high number of divorces.[28]

Another means of determining the relationship between the woman's age at marriage and divorce in the marriage loan cohort is to compare the mean or median age at marriage in those marriages which lasted until the woman reached 45 years of age with those which were dissolved by divorce. Marriages dissolved by death have also been considered.

The figures in Table 8 clearly indicate that the wife's age at marriage in the

---

[25] The Swedish population registers on the local level are kept by the Church of Sweden for each parish; the exceptions are Stockholm and Gothenburg, where the population registers are kept by the tax authorities. Registers from 110 parishes were used in this investigation.

[26] SOS: Folkmängden och dess förändringar 1966. Table 3.7: Mean, median and quartile age at first marriages and remarriages of husband and wife.

[27] SOS: Folkmängden och dess förändringar 1966. Table 3.22: Relative number of divorces in each marriage cohort by number of years after marriage.

[28] SOS: Befolkningsrörelsen. Översikt för åren 1951–1960. Table 14: Divorces by paragraph in the law by region. — The total number of divorces in the city of Stockholm is higher than the total number for all Swedish rural areas (21 450 and 20 728). Unfortunately, no information on a regional basis exists for marriage cohorts.

Table 8. *Mean and median age at marriage for women in the marriage loan cohort. Complete marriages and marriages dissolved by death or divorce*

Type	Number	Mean	Median
Complete marriages	207	24 yrs 4 months	23 yrs 3 months
Divorces	76	23 yrs 8 months	23 yrs 0 months
Deaths	20	24 yrs 0 months	23 yrs 6 months

cohort was not correlated to the rate of divorce. Although the divorce rate was high among couples in the marriage loan cohort and thus negatively affected fertility, this was not due to a lowering of the age at marriage but rather to other socio-economic factors (see below).

Marriage Loans and Legitimation of Children

The report of the Social Board assumed that the loans would encourage marriages between parents already having or expecting children. In the Stockholm cohort 5.3 per cent of the couples had children before marriage, and in 23.5 per cent of the marriages there was premarital conception. The number of children born before marriage and legitimated was thus small. Although the number of premarital conceptions may seem high, it was low compared to premarital conceptions among all marriages during the period in question; more than one-third of all marriages involved premarital conception.[29] It might, however, also be possible that the rate of premarital conceptions was different within the social strata from which the borrowers were recruited.

Premarital conception may also be an important factor with regard to age at marriage.[30] The median age at marriage for pregnant brides in the cohort was 22 years and 10 months. While this is somewhat lower than that of the total cohort (23.3), the difference is too small to allow any definite conclusions to be drawn.

Fertility Patterns in the Marriage Loan Cohort

Was lower age at marriage for women in the cohort related to an increase in the number of children born into a marriage? This was the intended result of the reform.

[29] Sjövall 1970, p. 3471, fig. 7 and 9 A.
[30] Sjövall and others represent the opinion that marriages with premarital conception are "forced" marriages and therefore, on average, show lower age at marriage. This opinion, which has proved not to be generally valid, might have been true for a society such as Sweden in the 1930's and 1940's. Cf. Kälvemark 1977: 3 and 1980.

Table 9. *Mean number of children per woman by age at marriage*

Age at marriage	15–19	20–24	25–29	30–34	35–39	40–44
	2.11	1.86	1.44	1.04	–	–

Table 10. *Mean number of children per marriage by type of marriage. Children born within the marriage loan cohort. Complete marriages, and marriages dissolved by divorce and death*

	Number	Number of children	Mean number of children/ family	Childless
Completed marriages	207	411	1.99	25 (12.1%)
Divorces	76	73	0.97	31 (40.8%)
Deaths	20	37	1.85	1
Total	303	521[a]		57 (18.8%)

[a] Five extramarital children, whose parents married later are included in this table.

Table 9 provides a measure of this by relating the average number of children born in a marriage to the age at marriage of the woman. The table indicates that an inverse correlation between the woman's age at marriage and the number of children born within the marriage did exist.[31] However, since it is not possible to establish with certainty whether or not the marriage loan reform actually did lower the age at marriage the effect of the reform on fertility remains unclear.

To further clarify this point the patterns of childbearing in the cohort will be examined. A total of 526 children were born in the 303 marriages of the cohort. The mean number of children per marriage is thus 1.7. The number is lower and seems to exclude any possibility that the marriage loans had an effect on fertility. However, since the fertility of women whose marriages ended in divorce is omitted the number of children per marriage is too low and does not provide an accurate measure of the fertility of the cohort.

An interesting point in Table 10 is the large number of childless marriages. These are too numerous to be explained only by sterility. In at least some of the marriages childlessness must have been due to deliberate family limitation.

[31] Bernhardt observed the same inverse correlation for the Swedish marriage cohorts of 1943–47. — Bernhardt 1971, pp. 74 ff., Table 4.4, pp. 77 ff.

Table 11. *Family patterns in the marriage loan cohort. Number of children. Complete marriages and marriages dissolved by divorce or death*

Number of children	0	1	2	3	4	5	6	Total
Complete marriages	25	47	71	41	17	5	1	207
Per cent	12.1	22.7	34.3	19.8	8.2	2.4	0.5	100
Divorces	31	25	14	4	2			76
Per cent	40.8	32.9	18.4	5.3	2.6			100
Deaths	1	9	6	2	1		1	20

Did the families have about the same number of children or was there a variation in family size? Table 11 shows that in "complete marriages", i.e. the marriages not dissolved by death or divorce before the wife reached 45 years of age, two children were most common with about one third of the marriages falling into this category. However, marriages resulting in one or three children were also fairly common. The marriages ending in divorce followed a different pattern with usually only one child being born.[32]

But even if only the complete marriages are considered, the average number of children is low.

Fertility by age and duration of marriage is presented in Table 12. Those who married early clearly had a higher fertility.

For the cohort as a whole, fertility declined with age. Total fertility was low, 97.8, which means that during a ten year period women in the cohort gave birth to on the average less than one child. The overwhelming proportion of the children were born during the first five years of the marriage with fertility declining rapidly with increased duration of marriage. Virtually no children were born after 20 years of marriage.

Family planning is also evident with regard to the spacing of the children. Whereas the average period between the marriage and the first child was 26 months for the complete marriages and the time between the first and the second child was 45 months the period between the third and the fourth child increased to 68 months. In marriages which ended in divorce the spacing of children was more concentrated: the first child was born after 20 months of marriage and the second after 35 months on an average. Marriages interrupted by death had a spacing pattern similar to that of complete marriages: the first child was born after 26 months of marriage and next child after 41 months.

[32] Cf. e.g. Cherlin 1977.

Table 12. *Marital fertility rates by age and duration of marriage. Number of children born per thousand woman-years* [a]

Age	Duration of marriage						
	0–4	5–9	10–14	15–19	20–24	25–29	Total
15–19	752.1						752.1
20–24	259.3	173.9					254.9
25–29	193.8	123.2	43.8				161.0
30–34	172.5	93.9	54.9	51.7			94.6
35–39	147.0	64.2	33.2	14.7			36.0
40–44			10.5	8.4			5.5
Total	223.8	98.9	37.8	12.1			97.8

[a] This means that if the value obtained is, e.g., 500 the women in question would have given birth to one child every other year on an average, 100 means that one child would have been born every tenth year, and the improbable number of 1 000 would mean that one child would have been born every year.—The calculations here are based on the number of months lived within marriage, which makes them more exact.

Table 13. *Parity progression ratios for the marriage loan cohort*

Children	0–1	1–2	2–3	3–4
Complete marriages	879	736	448	383
Divorces	592	422	316	–
Total	812	663	423	391

The same pattern emerges in the parity progression ratios presented in Table 13. Marriages dissolved by death are not shown separately, since they were too few to allow meaningful calculations.

The parity progression ratios are low for the marriage loan cohort underlining the fact that fertility was low. Fertility was lower in the cohort than in Swedish marriage cohorts in general during the same period. The effect of the marriage loans on fertility was thus negligible.[33]

Fertility and Social Status

A homogeneous pattern of low fertility has been observed for the marriage loan cohort as a whole. Were there any differences in the number of children per

[33] Cf. Table 5.

Table 14. *Average number of children per marriage by social status*

	Number of marriages	Number of children	Children/marriage
I	73	135	1.8
II	129	215	1.7
III	101	171	1.7

I = higher civil servants, people with higher education, owners of business enterprises, etc.
II = skilled workers, lower civil servants, salaried employees, etc.
III = unskilled workers, etc.

family on the basis of social status? To determine this the cohort has been divided into three groups on the basis of the occupation of the husband in each marriage: (I) persons with higher education, higher civil servants, owners of business enterprises, etc. (II) lower civil servants, skilled workers, etc. and (III) unskilled workers and persons in similar positions.[34] The mean number of children for each group is shown in Table 14.

The mean number of children per family is almost identical for all three social groups indicating that fertility level was independent of social status in the marriage loan cohort.

Geographical Structure and Fertility

In Sweden, regional differences in fertility were considerable during the period in question with Stockholm showing a low level of fertility. The generally low fertility in the marriage loan cohort thus compares well with Stockholm.

Hypothetically one might assume that people who were born and reared in an area with a certain family pattern would retain this pattern even after moving to another region. People born in another part of Sweden and moving to Stockholm could therefore be expected to have a higher fertility than people born in Stockholm, since fertility in the capital was among the lowest in the country. To determine if this was the case in the marriage loan cohort couples in the cohort were divided into four groups by place of birth according to whether husband, wife, both or neither had been born in Stockholm.

The regional influence of fertility seems to be confirmed, especially with regard to complete marriages, where disturbances in the family pattern due to divorce or death are eliminated. In Group I (both parents were born in Stockholm) the mean number of children per family is 1.6, whereas in the

[34] The stratification is based on the three so-called "social groups" that were then used in the official statistics.

Table 15. *Parents' birthplaces and fertility. The marriage loan cohort*

	Number of marriages	Per cent	Number of children	Mean number of children per family
Group I				
Complete marriages	42	73.7	68	1.6
Divorces	11	19.3	16	1.5
Deaths	4	7.0	5	1.3
Group II				
Complete marriages	45	69.2	96	2.1
Divorces	17	26.2	14	0.8
Deaths	3	4.6	11	3.7
Group III				
Complete marriages	28	53.8	59	2.1
Divorces	21	40.4	20	1.0
Deaths	3	5.8	4	1.3
Group IV				
Complete marriages	92	71.3	188	2.0
Divorces	27	20.9	23	0.8
Deaths	10	7.8	18	1.8

Group I   = both husband and wife born in Stockholm.
Group II   = husband born in Stockholm.
Group III   = wife born in Stockholm.
Group IV   = both husband and wife born outside Stockholm.

other groups the mean is 2.1 and 2.0. This further illustrates the traditionally low fertility of Stockholm. However, it must be pointed out that a confirmation of the hypothesis would require more research on regional fertility and how fertility patterns are changed or preserved when people move from one area to another.

The Deviating Families

A few families in the marriage loan cohort, however, differed from the general pattern. 27 families (nine per cent) had more than three children. How did their marriage and family patterns compare to patterns of the cohort in general?

Five of the 27 families had children before marriage—proportionally more than in the total cohort (5.3 per cent). In eight of the families the bride was

80

pregnant which was also relatively more than in the entire cohort. Five divorces occurred among these families, fewer in comparison to the cohort in general. Finally, the median age at marriage for women was 21.8, lower than for all women in the cohort.

Stratified into the three social groups used above, these families showed the same pattern, i.e., each group had very nearly the same share as in the whole cohort. The mean number of children is the same for all three groups (4.3). Children born prior to marriage and premarital conceptions were more frequent in groups II and III than in group I (11 and 2 respectively).

This small deviating group of families is of interest because they actually conformed, with regard to age at marriage, legitimation of children through marriage, and family size to the expected results of the marriage loan reform.

Social Aspirations, Marriage Loans and Family Planning

How, then, is the low fertility pattern of the cohort to be explained? The low level of fertility in the cohort was probably partly a reflection of the generally low fertility in Stockholm. This does not, however, provide a sufficient explanation for the somewhat ironic circumstance that the marriage loan borrowers in Stockholm behaved in a manner exactly reverse of that expected by the promoters of the policy.

A possible explanation might be found in the stipulations of the marriage loan reform. The borrowers—controlled by a local agent—had to be employed or be able to cite other conditions which indicated that they could repay the loans. They should also in the words of the regulations be "known as steady and economically prudent" and if possible have "shown a willingness to save". The very regulations for the granting of loans point towards a selection of people with a sense of economic rationality. Their fertility pattern with few children born early in marriage and with increasing intervals between births points to an ability to carry out a consistent family planning. The borrowers were thus people who could plan for the future.

Social and economic theories on fertility suggests that groups with strong social or economic aspirations or preferences would be more likely to use family planning than groups lacking these traits. These theories also imply that the individual members of such groups plan their futures in a long-term perspective.[35] As the loans were meant particularly for the lower middle class/upper working-class strata—precisely those social groups where one

[35] Planning and time horizons in connection with family planning will be treated more thoroughly in the following chapters. On these problems generally, see Odén 1975.

would expect the kind of social aspirations which would result in a family pattern characterised by few children—the low fertility level in the cohort is not unexpected.

An important problem remains. Are these results valid for the Swedish marriage loans in general? Is it possible to draw conclusions of a more general nature from the family pattern of the 303 Stockholm couples investigated here? As the sample was taken from an urban area with low fertility and by far the greatest share of the loans went to urbanised and industrialised areas, it would seem fairly safe to assume that the effect of the loans on fertility was negligible in other parts of the country as well.

How Well Informed Were the Politicians? Knowledge and Notions Behind the Swedish Decision on Marriage Loans

The success of pronatalist reforms intended to affect nuptiality is inversely correlated with the use of family planning in a population. As shown above, the marriage loan reform was directed at that part of the Swedish population where it was most likely to fail. This fact actualises questions about the reasoning and motives behind the decision on the loans. How well informed were the politicians and experts? What were, according to them, the causes of the fertility decline and how much did they know about current marriage and family patterns? And finally, what conclusions did they draw from such knowledge?

Motives other than pronatalist ones might have influenced the politicians in their decision on the marriage loans. It was a comparatively inexpensive measure though still spectacular from a population policy point of view, as well as being well suited to the prevalent policy of stimulating the economy by an increasing consumption financed by a deficit balancing of the national budget. The openly stated reasons for establishing the loans are of specific interest in this context, however.

As mentioned above, the political parties were not in agreement as to the reasons for the fertility decline in Sweden. The Conservatives on one hand saw an increased standard of living as the main cause; the parties on the left on the other hand maintained that it was caused by the current serious economic crisis. The Liberals tried to include both of these contrasting views in their interpretation; in a short-term perspective the decline was aggravated by the crisis, but in a long-term perspective it had to be seen as a reflection of the on-going radical social and economic transformation of Swedish society.[36]

[36] MFK 1935:1 and 230, FK 1935, p. 75 and 77. The National Group also stressed the importance of the economic crisis.

Alva and Gunnar Myrdal in their book *Kris i befolkningsfrågan* linked the fertility decline with an increased standard of living, but in a manner very different from the Conservatives. According to the Myrdals, an improvement in the standard of living, particularly among the working-class, could be attained, and once attained maintained only by keeping fertility far below unity. In other words, the Myrdals saw family limitation and the consequent fertility decline as a prerequisite for, not an effect of an improved standard of living.[37]

Regardless of the specific causes given for the decline in fertility, the parties generally agreed that economic and social change, whether recent or long-term, was accompanied by an increased use of birth control and by a new family pattern with small families.

The connection between an increased standard of living and fertility decline was also stressed in the report on marriage loans by the Committee on Population. The reasoning understandably is similar to that of the Myrdals. According to the report, childlessness within the working-class enabled a rather good standard of living—the wife in a childless marriage did not have to work outside the home and could devote all of her time to "the home of the lonely couple". A family with only one child could also uphold a decent standard, but already with the second child this became increasingly difficult, the difficulties increasing with each new child.[38] The precarious situation of salaried employees, students and other members of the middle classes was also stressed.

The demographer Sven Wicksell, referred to in the introduction to this chapter, in a memorandum in the Committee's report considered that low marriage rates and high ages at marriage for women were the main *causes* of the fertility decline in Sweden.[39] A natural consequence of this assumption was the proposal of measures intended to affect nuptiality. Wicksell regarded a lowering of the age at marriage for women in Sweden to the same level as in, for example, Denmark as probably sufficient for solving the entire population problem. But there was, of course, a fatal flaw in this kind of thinking, apparent in the very data on Swedish fertility Wicksell presented in the memorandum. He expressed some confusion over the fact that except for the northernmost parts of the country fertility was high where marriage rates were low and vice versa. This pattern persisted even when differences in age structure were taken into consideration. He also observed that the marriage rate was highest in the urban areas—where fertility was low. He did not,

[37] A. and G. Myrdal 1934.
[38] SOU 1936:14, the introduction.
[39] Wicksell 1936.

however, draw the correct conclusion that nuptiality had been replaced by birth control as the main regulator of fertility in Swedish society.[40]

Wicksell—and the other politicians and experts involved in the policy-making—were obviously well aware of the radical change in fertility patterns that had taken place in Sweden since the final decades of the 19th century. But when proposing measures to increase fertility, the politicians and experts assumed that marriage was still the main regulator of fertility. They were not able to draw the right conclusions based on their knowledge of the changing relationship between marriage and fertility. Since the loans were intended for precisely those groups in society who probably were among the earliest and most consistent appliers of birth control, the failure was further aggravated.

To be effective the loans should have been made available to those (such as the poor and unemployed in northern Sweden) who were least likely to limit their family size by birth control. That the loans would have been most effective as a pronatalist measure if the ages of marriage in such a population had been lowered strikingly illuminates their essential incompatibility with the concept of voluntary parenthood. Had the loans been effective they would certainly have resulted in non-planned and possibly unwanted children. But according to the principle of voluntary parenthood adopted by the Committee on Population, the only acceptable goal of a pronatalist policy was to make it possible for people to have the children they wanted. Had the loans been successful from a pronatalist point of view, the conflict between population policy and social policy goals would certainly have come to the fore.

[40] On the role of marriage as a regulator of fertility in earlier European demographic development and later its transformation see e.g., Laslett 1976 and Schofield 1976. For Sweden, see Kälvemark 1978.

Chapter 4

Maternity Relief Instead of Abortion

Introduction

Two population policy measures introduced in Sweden in 1937 provided for economic help during pregnancy and at childbirth. The first, a so-called maternity bonus, was to supplement help provided by a system handled by sickness insurance funds. Women who were uninsured and whose family income did not exceed 3 000 Sw. crowns a year were to receive a bonus of 75 Sw. crowns. The second measure, the so-called maternity relief or aid to destitute mothers, was intended for mothers who were in "obvious need" of economic help at childbirth. In this case up to 300 Sw. crowns could be granted.[1]

In an international perspective economic support at childbirth was generally provided by privately financed sickness insurance funds. Those who were uninsured and in need of help were generally forced to apply for poor relief. The supplementing of this type of system with a publicly financed maternity bonus and maternity relief was, at the time, unique to Sweden.[2]

Although the political discussions concerning both measures will be reviewed, this chapter will focus on the new and economically more important measure of maternity relief. As was the case with the marriage loan reform, the available sources permit an investigation of the entire process from political reasoning behind the decision to introduce maternity relief to effects of the reform.

Both policies aimed at helping *mothers* and both granted assistance on an one-time basis. The maternity relief, however, also had a special policy content. Women in particularly difficult circumstances were to be helped.

By improving conditions and care at childbirth these measures were to facilitate the birth of children. Such measures are positive counterparts of such repressive measures as preventing birth control and prohibiting abortions. The connection between repressive measures on one hand, and positive, voluntary ones on the other is clearly discernible in the reasoning behind the maternity

[1] SFS 1937: 339, 847 and 848.
[2] Cf. above ch. 1, p. 33.

relief. Alva Myrdal expressed it in the following manner: "The country could hardly as a democracy make the public confession that the advent of a child would be such a misfortune that the nation could find no other way out than by permitting the destruction of the fetus" ... And accordingly "it could not be accepted that the bearing of a child should mean economic distress to anybody in a country that is not poor and that wants children".[3] A country that refused abortions was thus morally obliged to create good conditions for *all* mothers and children.

The Abortion Committee

A special committee, appointed by the Ministry of Justice in 1934, was to prepare a new law on abortion.[4] Although this problem was not specifically treated by the Committee on Population, it was, however, asked to comment upon the report prepared by the Abortion Committee. This did not mean that population policy motives were absent in the work of the Abortion Committee. On the contrary, the committee pointed out that the recent favourable attitudes toward birth control among the population meant that it "has gone far beyond the dimensions called for by a feeling of responsibility for the welfare of the coming generation".[5] This attitude had also led to an increased willingness to accept abortion, and as far as it was possible to judge, the number of illegal abortions was steadily increasing.

The Abortion Committee did, however, propose that abortions be permitted not only on the more generally accepted medical, eugenic and humanitarian grounds (pregnancies by rape, etc.), but also on specific social grounds. Where the mother was exhausted, where the family was living in extreme poverty or where the pregnancy might significantly damage the woman's future career (e.g., preventing her from completing her education), abortions should not be considered as criminal. Furthermore, abortions would be permitted when a pregnancy resulted in social disgrace (as for unmarried mothers) or threatened a permanent relationship (e.g., pregnancy as a result of marital infidelity).

The Abortion Committee thus not only went beyond contemporary legal requirements for abortions in Sweden, but also those in force in other countries. As mentioned above, the Soviet Union was the only country which had accepted free abortions, though stricter legislation was again introduced in the middle of the 1930's. The committee—although being aware of the current population situation—did not accept the premise that low fertility should lead

[3] A. Myrdal 1941, p. 324.
[4] The work and proposals of the Abortion Committee are analysed in Hatje 1974 and Liljeström 1974.
[5] Cited in Liljeström 1974, p. 34.

to continued repressive abortion legislation. Seen in the contemporary social and political perspective, the proposal was radical. It also fitted well into the concept of voluntary parenthood launched by the Myrdals. They too had accepted that certain social conditions necessitated abortion.

But the proposal did not meet with success. And it did not meet with approval by the Committee on Population, a circumstance of particular interest in this context. In its official comments on the proposal the Committee on Population subscribed to the generally accepted humanitarian, eugenic and medical reasons for abortion. But an acceptance of the social causes would "mean expressly writing into the law a declaration of incompetence on the part of society to come to grips with the obvious and admittedly difficult social conditions ..."[6] This reasoning coincides with that of Alva Myrdal cited above. Children should be welcome in a country with a low birth rate, unmarried mothers should be socially accepted and the unpleasant facts of economic poverty and social distress be done away with.

In a way this argument lays considerable emphasis on appearances. To save face, Sweden a modern, democratic society, should not reveal its shortcomings. The argument is also strangely illogical. It states that no really democratic country can accept that its social and economic conditions are so bad that women have to choose abortions instead of having children. Thus it prohibits abortions. But the logical consequence is that in such a country no prohibition of abortions is necessary, since its social and economic conditions are *by definition* good. For such a country to prohibit abortions would result in exactly what the Committee on Population wished to avoid—the announcement that social and economic conditions in Sweden for mothers and children could be bad.

The new law was passed in 1938 and met with virtually no opposition in the *riksdag*, since it only recognised accepted humanitarian, eugenic and what was termed mixed social-medical requirements for abortion. The latter "when due to disease, malformation or weakness of the mother, the advent of the child would mean serious danger to her life or health".[7]

The concept of voluntary parenthood introduced by the Myrdals and adopted by the Committee on Population called for an abolishment of the current prohibition on the sale and distribution of contraceptives. Its comments on the Abortion Committee's report, on the other hand, were in direct contradiction to the idea of voluntary parenthood. It has already been argued that this contradictory attitude of the Population Committee was also apparent, although in a somewhat different manner, in the debate on the marriage loan reform.

[6] *Ibid.*, p. 41.
[7] *Ibid.*, p. 43.

Maternity Bonus and Maternity Relief:
Social Versus Population Policy Motives

Although the pronatalist motives behind the new abortion law outweighed the social motives, the social reasons for the prohibition of abortion underlined the moral obligation of Swedish society to help mothers and children in difficult conditions. The maternity bonus and maternity relief reforms, although actualised for pronatalist reasons, were thus strongly influenced by social motives. It is, therefore, of interest to examine the two measures more closely in order to distinguish between social and pronatalist motives.

In this respect there was an important difference between maternity bonus and maternity relief. According to the report from the Committee on Population every woman who had a child, regardless of her income or that of her husband, was to receive a maternity bonus.[8] A maternity bonus of this type might be considered as a premium for childbearing, or as the Social Board tartly remarked in its somewhat negative comment on the report, "motherhood must not be regarded as a means of making money".[9] Although an upper income limit was adopted by the *riksdag*, it was a generous one and in practice meant that about 90 per cent of all mothers would receive the bonus.

Although the direct and indirect pronatalist motives behind the maternity bonus were strong, social motives were also important. In the original motions on the problem in the *riksdag* in 1935 the pronatalist reasoning was all but absent.[10]

Social motives were also important with regard to the maternity relief reform, where the indirect argumentation that a restrictive abortion law was a rationale for social reforms received its full expression. It must be pointed out, however, that some of the institutions and organisations that were asked to publicly comment upon the committee's proposal on maternity relief were highly critical. Maternity relief, they argued, would only benefit the racially or otherwise less valuable parts of the population. It was therefore not a desirable measure from the population policy point of view.[11] The argument is the same as in the case of the marriage loan reform, which was regarded by some of its proponents as desirable precisely because it would increase fertility among what they considered as the most valuable section of the population. However, such views were exceptions. There was a general agreement with the conclu-

---

[8] SOU 1936:15. Cf. also Hatje 1974, p. 33.

[9] Comments on the proposal of the Committee on Population. (In *Prop.* 1937:38, pp. 30 ff.)

[10] MAK 1935:131, 196. A motion in 1937 by leading members of the Conservative party stressed the pronatalist policy motives behind maternity bonus and maternity relief. They demanded, however, a lower income limit than the one proposed. MFK 1937:203. MAK:406.

[11] Comments on the proposal of the Committee on Population. (In *Prop.* 1937:38, pp. 330 ff.)

sion of the Committee on Population that the economic and social conditions of many Swedish mothers were severe and ought to be relieved.[12]

In this context the social motives of the Committee on Population were clear: although relief should only be given to mothers in "obvious need" of help it should not be identified with poor relief. This was seen as a first step on the path to convincing people that social policy was not humiliating charity but a civic right.

Maternity Relief: Stipulations and Organisation

According to the 1937 ordinance on maternity relief the applicants could receive, for strictly specified purposes such as clothing, special food, dental care, help at home and so forth, a maximum allowance of 300 Sw. crowns. In some cases it was to be regarded as an interest-free loan. Women who were in the permanent care of the local poor relief authorities were not eligible for maternity relief—the underlying reasoning, as expressed by the Minister of Social Affairs, was that governmentally financed maternity relief should not replace the locally financed poor relief.[13] It is worth noticing in this context that social policies financed by the state were something new; poor relief and social welfare were traditionally the responsibility of the local municipalities.

Maternity Assistance Boards, one in each county council district, were created to handle maternity relief. These boards consisted of three members; two appointed by the central government and one by the county council. Applications for maternity relief were to be submitted to the local Child Welfare Committees, who appraised each application and recommended the amount and nature of the help to be given. The local Child Welfare Committees were also to execute the decisions of the Maternity Assistance Boards and ensure that the help was used in the stipulated way. Complaints against the decisions of these boards were reviewed by the Swedish Social Board.[14] As with the other measures proposed by the Committee on Population, maternity relief was mainly paid in kind.[15]

By allowing the Child Welfare Committees instead of the Public Assistance Boards to handle maternity relief on the local level, it was hoped that the measure would not be considered a form of poor relief. On the other hand, the

[12] *Ibid.*, pp. 30 ff.
[13] SFS 1937: 339. *Prop.* 1937: 38.
[14] SFS 1937: 339.
[15] Cf. Hatje 1974, p. 42 and 203 f. In particular Alva and Gunnar Myrdal advocated help in kind. Their argument was that help in cash would just become a part of a general family budget and not benefit the specific recipients of the different policies. See A. Myrdal 1941, pp. 133 ff.

strict regulations and control associated with the measure probably counter-acted these efforts to remove the stigma of poor relief.

Implementation

On the basis of a prediction that about 10 000 women a year would receive an average sum of 200 Sw. crowns each as maternity relief a total of one million Sw. crowns was tentatively granted for the first six month period of the reform (January through June 1938). The number of recipients was grossly under-estimated. During the first half of 1938 the Maternity Assistance Boards paid out 2.9 million Sw. crowns as maternity relief.[16] During the second half of 1938 this sum amounted to nearly 4 million Sw. crowns and by the end of 1938 the total number of recipients had reached no less than 34 263, or more than three times the predicted number. Although there was some variation, the average amount granted was approximately 200 Sw.crowns.[17]

In 1939 the number of granted applications rose to more than 45 000 and continued to rise reaching a high of over 65 000 granted applications in 1946 (Table 16). As a per cent of number of total births a peak was reached, however, already in 1941, the only year when more than half of all Swedish women who bore children received maternity relief. Seen against the original calculations of the decision-makers this is a remarkably high figure. Up to 1948 nearly half of all Swedish women who bore children were considered as being in "obvious need of help" by local and county council authorities. After 1948 there was a decline in the number of applications, which according to the Social Board, was due to a general rise in the standard of living.[18]

Administratively the implementation of the policy was very efficient and information concerning maternity relief seems to have spread with remarkable promptness. On the other hand, the gap between the amount preliminarily granted by the *riksdag* and the sum finally paid out during the first year of the reform indicates a discrepancy between the assumed situation and the actual situation. Was knowledge of current economic and social conditions in Sweden insufficient among experts and decision-makers? Or did the authorities adopt a too liberal interpretation of the concept of "obvious need of help"?

The considerable overdraft of the original grant caused reactions from various quarters—the Social Board, the Ministry of Social Affairs and the National Accounting and Audit Bureau. In the autumn of 1938 the Social

---

[16] *Konferens i Stockholm etc.*, p. 3.
[17] *Sociala Meddelanden* 1939, 5, p. 337.
[18] *Mödrahjälpen under år 1949.* (*Sociala Meddelanden* 1950: 7.) *Mödrahjälpen under år 1956.* (*Sociala Meddelanden* 1957: 7.)

Table 16. *Maternity relief 1939–1956*

Year	Total number of applications N	Total number of applications As a per cent of births	Number granted N	Number granted As a per cent of births	Amount granted	Amount granted Average per case
1939	–	–	45 726	47.0	8 805 000	190
1940	–	–	42 178	44.0	6 922 000	162
1941	–	–	50 071	50.2	8 899 000	176
1942	–	–	53 681	47.1	10 022 000	186
1943	68 238	45.4	56 489	45.0	10 604 000	187
1944	76 002	56.3	63 745	47.2	12 562 000	197
1945	75 896	56.1	64 849	47.9	13 527 000	208
1946	76 977	58.1	65 249	49.5	14 682 000	225
1947	71 597	54.4	60 798	47.2	14 229 000	234
1948	67 570	53.5	53 503	42.3	12 549 000	235
1949	61 463	50.8	47 690	39.4	11 347 000	238
1950	58 501	50.8	44 976	39.0	10 774 000	240
1951	51 498	46.8	36 304	33.0	8 760 000	241
1952	48 447	44.0	33 152	30.1	8 262 000	249
1953	46 249	42.0	31 408	28.5	8 772 000	279
1954	41 577	39.6	28 484	27.1	8 960 000	315
1955	32 589	30.4	19 578	18.2	5 686 000	290
1956	28 556	26.4	17 558	16.2	5 635 000	321

Source: Sociala Meddelanden 1957, 7, p. 467.

Board organised a conference for the Maternity Assistance Boards.[19] The meaning given to "in obvious need of help" as a criterion for maternity relief was discussed. It was found that various interpretations were used by the different boards, for example the use of specific income limits, consideration of the number of children in the family, etc.

A general income limit was proposed to replace individual assessments of the degree of need, but met with opposition. Closely related to the interpretation of "in obvious need of help" was the delimitation between poor relief and maternity relief. As mentioned above, the Minister of Social Affairs specifically prescribed that maternity relief should not be given to persons who where continuously receiving poor relief. This decision was taken because it was suspected that the local authorities might try to improve their economic situation by replacing poor relief with maternity relief.

[19] *Konferens i Stockholm etc.*

To avoid such misuse of maternity relief by the municipalities, the Social Board demanded that the ordinance be changed so that maternity relief could be given to those receiving poor relief.[20] But the Minister of Social Affairs explained that this clause only concerned women who were continuously taken care of by the Public Assistance Boards.[21] This statement was interpreted by the National Assistance and Child Welfare Officer as implying that there was no legal hindrance to granting both maternity relief and poor relief to other women. Therefore the local Public Assistance Boards were admonished to ensure that maternity relief did not replace poor relief in such a way as to damage the interests of the recipient.[22]

The National Accounting and Audit Bureau in 1939 also conducted an investigation of maternity relief and found fault with the differences in the amount of maternity relief granted and the lack of conformity in the handling of applications.[23] Deficiencies in the accounts of the local Child Welfare Committees were criticised, as well as their way of controlling the recipients' use of any money granted. In some cases women were accused of having bought other than the permitted items, for example, household articles, furniture, and coffee. The criterion "in obvious need of help" was found by the bureau to be too vague, and a more precisely defined income limit was recommended.

In November 1939 the Minister of Social Affairs commissioned the Social Board to conduct a special investigation of maternity relief and the way it was handled by the regional and local authorities.[24] This was undertaken partly because of the negative report issued by the National Accounting and Audit Bureau. In its report the Social Board to some extent defended the Maternity Assistance Boards and the Child Welfare Committees, remarking, for example, that after the initial years of relative inexperience, deficiencies had largely disappeared. The positive aspects of maternity relief were strongly emphasised and the demands for stricter criteria of need were rejected.

In 1940 the income limit for maternity bonus was lowered from 3 000 to 2 500 Sw. crowns a year.[25] The ordinance on maternity relief remained

---

[20] *Meddelanden från Kungl. Socialstyrelsens byrå för fattigvårds- och barnavårdsärenden m. m.*, 1939: 76, p. 2. A member of the Communist party introduced a private bill in the *riksdag* with similar demands, but it was rejected. (MAK 1939: 47.)

[21] *Statsverkspropositionen* 1939, V, p. 30.

[22] *Meddelanden från Kungl. Socialstyrelsens byrå för fattigvårds- och barnavårdsärenden m. m.* 1939: 76, pp. 1 ff. In a circular to the Maternity Assistance Boards the Social Board also drew their attention to the circumstance that maternity relief must not replace poor relief. (*Riksdagens revisorers berättelse, del II: Förklaringar*, p. 5. In *Bihang till lagtima riksdagens protokoll* 1940: 2: 1.)

[23] *Riksdagens revisorers berättelse, del I*, pp. 23 ff.

[24] See *Prop.* 1940 (*lagtima riksdagen*): 5, p. 13.

[25] SFS 1940: 552.

essentially the same, although the control regulations became stricter.[26] The debated criterion "in obvious need of help" remained unchanged.

Whether the local Child Welfare Committees tried to replace locally financed poor relief with maternity relief or not, it is clear that the governmentally financed maternity relief, which implied no financial cost for the local municipalities, made it easier for them to be liberal in recommending that applications be granted. This circumstance might at least partly explain the rapid diffusion of information on maternity relief among potential applicants, particularly in those parts of Sweden where economic conditions were bad and where, accordingly, poor relief was a burden on the local budget. As will be shown in the following, the regional distribution of maternity relief grants coincides with geographic differences in economic conditions.

Regional Distribution

Maternity relief grants as a per cent of live births showed considerable geographic variation (Map 5). In 1938 Halland *län* in the south of Sweden showed the lowest figure with 20 per cent, whereas Norrbotten *län* in the very north showed the highest—81 per cent. In 1939 Örebro *län* in the middle of Sweden had the lowest percentage of granted applications and Västerbotten *län* in the north of Sweden the highest. Despite the general increase in the number of grants during 1939, differences between the regions remained relatively constant; the same nine county council districts showed the highest figures for both years.

Although most Maternity Assistance Boards granted about 90–95 per cent of the submitted applications, there were some differences. For example, the board in Örebro *län* only granted between 75 and 80 per cent of the applications.[27] Different policies in this respect can, however, only explain a small part of the over-all differences. The Social Board in the above-mentioned investigation suggested two possible explanations. Since the number of unmarried mothers is relatively high among the recipients a variation in the illegitimacy rate is a possible explanation.[28] When regional differences in illegitimacy are standardised, the variations in maternity relief decrease to some extent, supporting the assumption of the Social Board.

---

[26] SFS 1940: 786. Complaints were later raised that the control function of the local Child Welfare Committees had become so dominant that it endangered their primary duty of seeing to the interests of the applicants for maternity relief. (Lannerberth 1941: 1 and 2.)

[27] *Riksdagens revisorers berättelse, del I*, pp. 28 f.

[28] *Undersökning rörande mödrahjälpen under första halvåret 1939.* In *Prop.* 1940 (*urtima riksdagen*): 5, bil. A. pp. 169 ff.

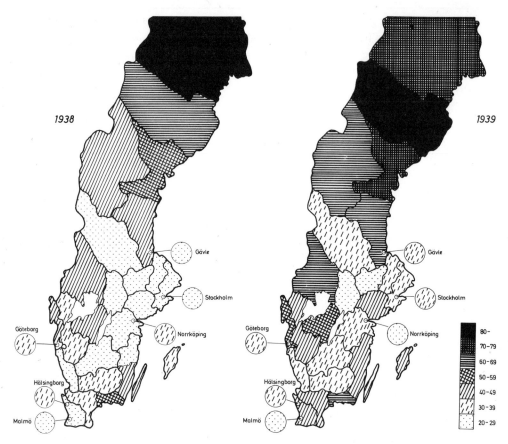

Map. 5. Maternity relief by county council districts. Granted relief in per cent of number of live births.

Source: Socialstyrelsens fjärde byrå: Mödrahjälpsstatistik, (SCB).

Another possible explanation of the regional variations in maternity relief could be that economic conditions in different parts of the country varied.[29] The northern parts of Sweden were heavily hit by the depression and unemployment rates were particularly high there, especially in lumbering and sawmill districts.[30] Moreover, farmers' holdings were small in northern Sweden and the rural population lived in generally poorer conditions than in other parts of the country.[31] As can be seen from Map 5, maternity relief grants as a percentage of live births were extremely high in northern Sweden, again

[29] *Ibid.,* p. 171.
[30] *Statistisk årsbok för Sverige* 1940.
[31] Cf. *Riksdagens revisorers berättelse, del II*, pp. 112, 114.

94

substantiating the assumptions of the Social Board. The map showing the regional distributions of maternity relief may also be considered as a map depicting regional differences in poverty and unemployment, a situation reflected in reports from the Maternity Assistance Boards.[32]

Against this background it seems as if the experts and decision-makers who estimated the amount of money needed to implement the reform had an insufficient knowledge of the actual economic conditions under which large parts of the Swedish population lived. Despite a liberal treatment of applications by the Child Welfare Committees and Maternity Assistance Boards, this underestimation of the actual need emerges as the main explanation of the difference between the amount tentatively granted and the amount actually granted.

This "over-implementation" of the original goals and estimates of maternity relief which affected nearly half of all Swedish women having children during the years in question may have increased the effects of the reform beyond all expectations. But before the effects of the maternity relief reform are analysed and discussed, various special features of the reform need to be further illuminated.

Maternity Relief—a Reform for Women

As has already been pointed out, maternity relief was one of the social policy measures financed by the central government instead of by the local governments, and efforts were made to avoid giving this reform the stigma attached to locally financed welfare and poor relief. But it was also new in quite another respect—it was a reform *intended for women*. Only women could apply and the help granted was exclusively meant for women and their new-born children, not for the rest of the family.

Reports bear witness to the novelty of giving the relief to married women and not to their husbands. Despite regulations in the ordinance to the contrary, the husband was allowed at times to collect the relief from the Child Welfare Committee.[33] Participants in the above-mentioned conference on maternity relief in 1938 testified to such experiences: "It is not a question of hardness or ill will on behalf of the men—it is just that it is all so completely at odds with general custom and tradition. Always earlier, in matters concerning money it has been the men's money."[34] Another participant said that "in

---

[32] *Ibid.*, pp. 1 ff. Cf. also *Konferens i Stockholm etc.* and *Undersökning rörande mödrahjälpen under första halvåret 1939.*

[33] *Konferens i Stockholm etc.*, pp. 17 ff. and *Riksdagens revisorers berättelse, del II*, pp. 128 f.

[34] *Konferens i Stockholm etc.*, p. 18.

many parts of the country, particularly in the countryside, it is still something unheard of that women could have money at their own disposal".[35]

The novelty of giving benefits directly to married women also explains in part why the grants was subject to control and why help was given in kind. In a situation where men customarily controlled the family's income and property, help in kind and/or under strict control was considered as a means of ensuring that the relief actually reached the intended recipients—the women and their new-born children.[36] Despite paternalistic and often degrading regulations and control, maternity relief was in many ways a radical reform. Maternity relief gave many women the opportunity to handle money and to use it for their own benefit. In various official reports on maternity relief, the positive experiences of women receiving help were often cited. Grateful letters and statements from women were also quoted and the fact that many women, for the first time since their marriage, received something new for themselves was repeatedly pointed out.[37] The social and economic effects generally were judged to be very positive.[38] But in this context it must be remembered that these reports came mainly from the authorities dealing directly with the relief and may therefore very likely be biased.

Maternity Relief: Recipients and Effects

Since nearly half of all Swedish women having children during the period in question received maternity relief, the intended effects of the measure might very well have been achieved. However, it is difficult to identify precisely what effects were intended, and consequently any clear, quantifiable analysis is impossible. The main, openly avowed reason for introducing the reform was to "soften-up" the restrictive law prohibiting abortions. This was done for ethical reasons and need for moral justification by the decision-makers and did not necessarily involve any other expected results.

Pronatalist intentions were thus indirect and for the main part closely related to the restrictions on abortion. However, some opinions expressed in the official comments on the proposition on maternity relief stressed pronatalist aspects.[39] Similar views were expressed in some of the official comments on the proposition on changes in the maternity relief ordinance in 1940, when the hoped for effect on illegal abortions did not appear. Furthermore numerous

---

[35] *Ibid.*, p. 19. Cf. also *Riksdagens revisorers berättelse, del II*, p. 80.

[36] *Konferens i Stockholm etc.*, pp. 17 ff. – Married women gained full legal rights in Sweden 1920.

[37] *Konferens i Stockholm etc.*, esp. p. 20. *Riksdagens revisorers berättelse, del II*, p. 109.

[38] *Konferens i Stockholm etc., passim. Riksdagens revisorers berättelse, del II, passim.*

[39] *Prop.* 1937:38, pp. 30 ff. and 78 ff.

unspecified pronatalist effects were suggested in support of maternity relief. In the proposition the Minister of Social Affairs also suggested that a decrease in maternity relief might have negative *psychological* effects, since a high level of relief indirectly supported a high psychological estimation of motherhood and childbearing.[40] Another form of pronatalist reasoning was that which considered maternity relief as positively affecting infant mortality. Although some such effect might have occurred, it is doubtful if it significantly influenced infant mortality rates since they were already low. The opinion that maternity relief in itself could be a means of inducing people to have more children, however, was nowhere openly expressed.

The most important population policy motive behind the maternity relief reform was of a qualitative nature. Maternity relief would help to improve conditions at childbirth and afterwards for both mother and child, and thereby improve the general quality of the Swedish population.[41] The qualitative element is also apparent in the concern of those people and institutions who worked with maternity relief over the fact that mothers labeled as "asocial" also received or might receive maternity relief. Expressed in population policy terms, it was thought, that the reform should not benefit any section of the population regarded as inferior or without value.[42]

The social effects of the maternity relief reform were those most often stressed by those who proposed the reform and later by those who enacted it. Indeed, the two *riksdag* motions originally demanding it were based almost exclusively on social arguments. It is, however, difficult to distinguish between the population policy and social policy intentions since they merged almost completely within the framework of the reform. The beneficial social effects of maternity relief were abundantly testified to—at least among the authorities who handled the relief.

Although maternity relief was considered as beneficial and reached a large number of women, its relationship to poor relief makes the establishment of its social and population policy effects difficult. As mentioned above the National Accounting and Audit Bureau questioned this aspect of the use of maternity relief. One way of establishing the extent that maternity relief was used as a substitute for poor relief, is to determine whether or not those women who received maternity relief were also those who usually received poor relief. Four municipalities in different parts of Sweden were tested in this respect and it was found that maternity relief was generally received by a much higher number of women than those who themselves, or whose families, were on poor

---

[40] *Prop.* 1940: 5 (*urtima riksdagen*), pp. 15 ff., p. 31, p. 73.
[41] SOU 1936: 15, pp. 36 ff. Cf. also A. Myrdal 1941, pp. 324 ff.
[42] *Prop.* 1937: 38. p. 30 f. *Prop.* 1940: 5 (*urtima riksdagen*), p. 73. *Konferens i Stockholm etc*, pp. 49 ff.

Table 17. *Marital status of applicants and recipients of maternity relief. Countryside and towns. January – June 1939*

	Married	Un-married	All	Unmarried in per cent of all recipients
Countryside				
Applicants	5 143	1 321	6 464	20.4
Recipients	4 743	1 263	6 006	21.0
Cities and Towns				
Applicants	1 413	579	1 992	29.1
Recipients	1 199	555	1 754	31.6
All				
Applicants	6 556	1 900	8 456	22.5
Recipients	5 942	1 818	7 760	23.4

Source: *Undersökning rörande mödrahjälpen under första halvåret 1939.* (In *Prop. 1940: 5, urtima riksdagen,* pp. 136–137.)

relief.[43] Although maternity relief was not always used in the way intended it is fairly clear that within a limited range social and qualitative population policy effects were achieved.

To be able to study the effects of the reform in a population policy context an examination of the recipients and especially their family patterns is necessary. It is important to remember in this context that the reform had the character of one-time benefit. It did not aim at the same kind of long-term effect as, for example, the marriage loan reform or the reform on improved housing for large families. It was meant as a temporary alleviation at an often particularly difficult time for both mothers and children.

The Investigation by the Social Board

The regional distribution of maternity relief and its relationship to geographical differences in economic development presented earlier was based on a report by the Social Board. Further information concerning the recipients is

[43] Investigations were made of maternity relief given out in Uppsala (Uppsala *län*), Mörbylånga (Kalmar *län*), Åmål (Älvsborg *län*) and Revsund (Jämtland *län*). For Uppsala information was obtained from the minutes of the Maternity Assistance Board (Uppsala County Council Archives) and the Public Assistance Board (Uppsala Municipal Archives); for the other areas the minutes of the Child Welfare Committees and the Public Assistance Boards in the respective municipal archives were used. More than eighty per cent of the maternity relief receivers had not recently been given poor relief.

Table 18. *Number of previous children among applicants and recipients of maternity relief. Countryside and towns. January–June 1939*

	Childless women	Women with 1–2 children	Women with 2 or more children	All
Countryside				
Applicants	1 557	2 077	1 509	5 143
Recipients in per cent of applicants	85.5	93.5	97.4	92.2
Towns				
Applicants	546	620	247	1 413
Recipients in per cent of applicants	80.1	85.2	93.1	84.9
All				
Applicants	2 103	2 697	1 756	6 556
Recipients in per cent of applicants	84.3	91.5	96.8	90.6

Source: *Undersökning rörande mödrahjälpen under första halvåret 1939.* (In *Prop. 1940: 5, urtima riksdagen*, p. 144.)

available in this report and will be presented below, but to adequately consider family patterns among those who received help a more in-depth investigation is necessary. Such an investigation has been carried out for all women applying for maternity relief in the town of Uppsala in 1938.

According to the study by the Social Board, which refers to the first half of 1939, more than one-fifth of the recipients were unmarried mothers.[44] A few widowed or divorced women were also included in this category. In the cities their share was nearly one-third of all recipients, whereas in the countryside it was only one-fifth (cf. Table 17). In 1939 nearly thirteen per cent of all women who gave birth were unmarried.[45] Not surprisingly this category was overrepresented among maternity relief applicants and recipients.

The number of previous children among the applicants for and recipients of maternity relief is presented in Table 18. Previous children were few among the unmarried mothers. Among the married women more than forty per cent had one or two children, and nearly thirty per cent had three children or more. A good thirty per cent had no children. Unfortunately, the figures only provide a rough estimate of family size since children older than sixteen years were not

[44] *Undersökning rörande mödrahjälpen etc.*, p. 134.
[45] *Historisk statistik för Sverige*, Table 28. Population changes 1749–1967.

99

Table 19. *Occupations amoung husband of married applicants and recipients of maternity relief, January–June 1939, compared to occupations among the total economically active population in 1940. Per cent*

	Husbands of maternity relief		Total economically active population in 1940
	Applicants	Receivers	
Agriculture	40.8	42.6	28.8
Industry	44.3	42.8	35.5
Commerce and transport	11.0	10.7	17.7
General administration, white-collar professions, public services, etc.	3.9	3.9	18.0
	100.0	100.0	100.0

Sources: *Undersökning rörande mödrahjälpen under första halvåret 1939.* (In *Prop. 1940: 5, urtima riksdagen*, p. 151), *Historisk statistik för Sverige. Del 1. Befolkning* (Stockholm 1967), Table 24.

included. As can be seen from Table 18, women with previous children tended to receive maternity relief somewhat more often than childless ones.[46]

Married applicants and recipients were also classified on the basis of the occupations of their husbands into occupational groups. About seventy per cent of the husbands were manual workers. Table 19 shows that those engaged in agriculture and those who worked in industry were overrepresented compared to the total population. Commerce and transport, general administration, white-collar professions and public services were on the other hand underrepresented.[47] As mentioned above, the share of unemployed or only temporarily employed was high among both applicants for and recipients of maternity relief during the first half of 1939.[48]

From the investigation of the Social Board it is clear that the family patterns of maternity relief applicants and recipients differed in certain important respects from those of the rest of the population. Nearly a third were unmarried mothers, compared to less than thirteen per cent in the total population. Although no comparable information on complete family size is available, it appears that married recipients had larger than average families. Furthermore, married recipients came mainly from families whose incomes were dependent

[46] *Undersökning rörande mödrahjälpen etc.*, pp. 143 ff.

[47] *Ibid.*, pp. 150 f.

[48] Cf. *Mödrahjälpen under år 1956.* (*Sociala Meddelanden* 1957: 7.)

100

on agriculture and industry. This plus the fact that unemployment was high among the recipients of maternity relief (about 20 %) indicate that these families were generally poorer and "in obvious need of help".

Maternity Relief: An In-depth Study of Family Patterns

In the preceding chapter it was shown that the marriage loan reform was directed towards a particular stratum of the population. A certain type of family pattern emerged, a pattern characterised by an ability for overall planning, a high motivation and an ability to limit family size, all of which were in conformance with the norms and values prevalent in the surrounding society.

Socially and economically maternity relief obviously aimed at other groups of the population. In contrast to the marriage loan reform, the regulations for maternity relief more openly selected certain types of families and family patterns. This was especially true in the case of unmarried mothers. Although never directly prescribed in the ordinance, maternity relief authorities showed an inclination to use a large family as one of the criteria for granting maternity relief.[49]

The two above-mentioned family pattern characteristics of maternity relief recipients can be deduced from the regulations in the maternity relief ordinance. But was maternity relief in practice also selective in other ways? To answer this question and to more closely establish the effects of the measure the previously mentioned in-depth study of women receiving maternity relief in Uppsala, a rather large but comparatively unindustrialised town about 50 miles to the north of Stockholm, will be considered.

Method and Population

Because of the temporary character and, accordingly, the temporary effect of maternity relief, this study is somewhat more limited in scope than those on marriage loans and housing for large families. Since those women who received maternity relief received it at different stages in their life and family cycles there is also less conformity among the population than in the studies of the other two population policy measures. Another special feature is that only here do unmarried mothers form a part of the population investigated.

The names of the recipients of maternity relief in Uppsala were obtained from the minutes of the regional Maternity Assistance Board. They were afterwards identified in the birth records and general population registers of the two parishes of Uppsala. All recipients were found and identified in the

---

[49] *Undersökning rörande mödrahjälpen etc.*, pp. 152 ff. *Konferens i Stockholm etc.*

population records, so there is no loss in this respect. Information was obtained on date of birth of the mother, date of marriage and family size. Occupational information was also obtained from the records; in the case of the married recipients this information refers only to the husband, since the wife's profession or occupation outside the home was not always given.

A control population was selected on the basis of a random sample from the birth records in 1938 for the two parishes. This sample was then located in the general parish registers and information on the same variables as for the maternity relief population was obtained.

In 1938 84 women were granted maternity relief in Uppsala, representing 15 per cent of all births that year. Twenty-three of the recipients were unmarried mothers (27 per cent). Compared to the rest of the country the percentage of those women who received maternity relief in the county council region of Uppsala was about average. The control group consists of 54 persons. Only six of these were unmarried (11 per cent). The figures on marital status therefore correspond well when compared to the country as a whole for both recipients and non-recipients.

Unmarried mothers

Were there any differences between the unmarried mothers who applied for maternity relief and received it, and those who did not? The median age at childbirth was the same for both groups, 22 years. There were some differences in the occupational structure of the two groups—although the control group is, of course, too small to allow any conclusions to be drawn. Eight among the maternity relief receivers but none in the control group were employed in domestic service. Other occupations such as factory work and public service were found in both groups.

There was another difference between the two groups which might be more important. Four of six in the control group, but only five out of the twenty-three in the maternity relief group married very soon after. This circumstance, together with what appears to be a somewhat better occupational situation, may explain why the six unmarried women in the control group did not apply for maternity relief.

Married women

The unmarried women who received maternity relief were young and at least for some of them the pregnancy in question was very likely an early stage in what later was a normal marriage. The married women, on the other hand, were more heterogeneous in this respect, since they included both women who were pregnant with their first child as well as women who already had given birth to several children.

Table 20. *Mean number of children by duration of marriage. Recipients of maternity relief and control group (Uppsala in 1938)*

	Duration of marriage				
	(0–1)	0–4	5–9	10–14	15-years–
Maternity relief group					
Mean number of children	(1.1)	1.3	2.7	4.2	5.5
Per cent of all marriages	(29.5)	62.3	18.0	9.8	9.8
Control group					
Mean number of children	(1.0)	1.1	1.8	2.0	–
Per cent of all marriages	(25.0)	77.1	18.8	4.2	–

The married recipients of maternity relief may be expected to have more children than the control group. Were they also at a later stage of their family cycle and thus on the average, also older? The median age of those recipients who gave birth in 1938 is 26, whereas it is as high as 30 for the control group. Corresponding mean values are 26.9 and 29.2 with a somewhat higher standard deviation for those receiving maternity relief—7.4 compared to 5.4.

The recipients of maternity relief were therefore considerably younger than the women in the control group. Can this be explained by younger ages at marriage and/or the fact that the recipients had their children in more rapid succession than women in the control group? Or were the recipients of maternity relief in Uppsala atypical in having fewer children than the general childbearing population?

The median age at marriage was 23 for the recipients and 26 for the control group. For many of them this was the first child—eighty-one per cent of the control group and seventy-two per cent of the recipients.

Family size is presented in Table 20. To allow comparisons between the two groups, they have been classified by duration of marriage. Those who had been married less than five years in 1938 form one group, those who had been married more than five but less than ten years another, etc. The mean number of children is given for each group.

Regardless of the length of the marriage the recipients of maternity relief had larger families on the average than the control group. They married earlier and had more children. Twenty-eight women (46 per cent) in the maternity relief group but only ten (21 per cent) in the control group were pregnant at marriage.

Table 21. *Mean number of children by duration of marriage. Twenty-nine marriages of lower social status within the control group. (Uppsala in 1938)*

	Duration of marriage			
	(0–1)	0–4	5–9	10–14-years
Mean number of children	(1.0)	1.0	2.5	2
Per cent of all marriages	(37.9)	82.8	13.8	3.5

That there tends to be a correlation between poverty and large families is well-known.[50] The people who benefited from the maternity relief obviously belonged to the poorer strata of the Swedish society. Large families, therefore, may be associated with poor economic and social circumstances even here. But was the family pattern of the recipients typical of their own social and economic stratum or did they differ in any respect?

To provide an answer to this question the recipients will be compared to those women in the control group who belonged to roughly the same social group, i.e., those in unskilled and semi-skilled occupations. It must, however, be stressed that since the application for and receiving of maternity relief in itself indicates a bad economic situation, it is very probable that the non-recipients within the same occupational group still had the advantage of a better economic position over the recipients. The construction of a completely corresponding control group is therefore not possible.

Twenty-nine women (60 per cent) of the 48 in the original control group were married to husbands with unskilled or semi-skilled occupations. Their median age at marriage was 25 years (mean value 25.7). Ten of them (34 per cent) were pregnant at marriage, which means that no premarital conceptions occurred in the higher social groups, where in all probability stricter sexual norms and social control prevailed. The mean number of children by duration of marriage is shown in Table 21. Since absolute number of cases in each group is small the results should be regarded as only tentative.

The family pattern which emerges for this sub-group of the control population seems to fall in between that of the recipients on one hand and the total control group on the other. Median age at marriage is higher than the 23 years for the recipients and lower than the 26 for the total control group. Premarital conception is frequent but not to the same extent as among the recipients. The mean number of children is slightly higher than for the total control group, but lower than for the recipients.

[50] Cf. for example, Rainwater 1960, Askham 1975.

Comparisons between the recipients of maternity relief and the smaller control group do not show radically different marriage and family patterns but rather two versions of the same pattern. In contrast to the higher social strata, here there is what might be called a working-class marriage and family pattern, characterised by lower ages at marriage, higher rates of premarital conception and more children. The lower ages at marriage and, above all, the frequent occurrence of premarital conceptions may be reflections of other sexual norms and possibly other functions of marriage than those found among the higher social strata.[51]

In comparison with the higher social strata, and also with, for example, the characteristics displayed by the recipients of marriage loans the differences may also be interpreted as reflecting variations in behaviour and attitudes. In particular, the characteristics may be seen as indicators of planning ability. Here the premarital conceptions are of interest. Can a correlation between a higher frequency of premarital conceptions and a higher number of children be used as an indicator of unplanned or less planned behaviour?

Non-planning or inconsistent planning may be seen as a function of shorter time perspectives and possibly also of a feeling of helplessness or of not being able to control one's own future—in all or some areas of life.[52] When there are no or only a few resources available for people to use in affecting their future, there seems little point in making plans. Lack of planning has also been associated with cultural characteristics as a function of the so-called poverty cultures, where behaviour and attitudes which perpetuate poverty are transferred from generation to generation.[53] A high rate of premarital conception would indicate an overall lack of planning and a short-term time perspective and in turn result in large families (at least if abortions are not available).

Conclusion

Maternity relief was probably selective of a certain fertility pattern, characterised by a comparatively low degree of planning and families larger than the average. Maternity relief was therefore given not only to a group with other characteristics and behaviour than those who received marriage loans, but also to that part of the population which actually contributed most to the biological reproduction of Swedish society. Maternity relief than certainly reached the

---

[51] Cf. Kälvemark 1978: 1.
[52] On planning and time horisons, see Odén 1975.
[53] Askham 1975 gives a survey and discussion of theories on poverty, poverty cultures and fertility.

right targets from a population policy point of view. In this context it is ironical that whereas the borrowers of marriage loans did not biologically reproduce themselves because of their conformance to the dominant norms and behaviour of the surrounding society, the maternity relief recipients filled these reproductive goals by *not* conforming to the very same norms and behaviour.[54]

[54] Cf. Elster 1973.

Chapter 5

Improved Housing for Large Families

Introduction

Large families were at the same time the goals and the targets for the pronatalist policies of the 1930's. Large—or at least larger families—were the ultimate goal, but even the already existing large families were considered important by the pronatalist policy makers. In various ways large families throughout Europe were given testimonials of approval and support by their governments. In France, Germany and Italy, for instance, large families were not only given special advantages but also spectacular premiums and medals; the parents of large families were held up as models for the nation.[1] Of particular interest were large families living in poor or difficult economic conditions; the presence of poverty among those on whom people were expected to model their family pattern in the future could not be accepted. It is here that the qualitative aspect becomes important. To improve living conditions for children in large families also meant an improvement in the quality of the population in general.

Bad housing and overcrowding were problems considered to have been particularly important in this context. In several countries—Belgium, France, Germany and Italy—efforts were made to provide families, and particularly large families, with decent housing. Preference was given to large families in providing accommodation in what is referred to as "cheap" or "popular" houses.[2] In Belgium, large families wanting to buy or build houses of their own

---

[1] Glass 1940, p. 172, pp. 237 ff., pp. 295 ff., p. 303, p. 453, p. 455. — In France a special *Médaille de la Famille* was awarded to mothers with at least five children. The medal was graded—bronze, silver and silver-gilt—in proportion to the number of children. In Germany, particularly high child allowances were given to families with five or more children. Children in large families also received special educational grants. Medals were also given to large German families, apparently in imitation of the French example. In Italy, large families (defined as families with seven or more children) received considerable tax deductions and also other advantages. — Newly married couples in Italy received a special book—*Libretto di famiglia*—containing pronatalist admonitions by Mussolini and 24 (!) blank pages intended for the birth certificates of children to be born into the new family. (Hamrin 1965, p. 78).

[2] Glass 1940, pp. 244 ff., p. 302, pp. 170 ff.

were given special consideration.[3] The extent to which the policies were implemented in practice is, however, difficult to determine—Belgium seems to have been that European country where such policies were most successful. In France and Belgium, however, housing reforms cannot be directly related to the population policy context of the 1930's, since they were mainly introduced during earlier periods.

In Sweden, an act issued in September 1935 decreed that publicly financed loans should be made available to build tenement houses in order to provide improved and cheap housing for large families with little means.[4] Contrary to similar schemes in other countries, this act specifically and exclusively concerned large families.

Improved Housing for Large Families: Stipulations and Background

The publicly financed loans for the building of these houses were supplemented by so-called family rent rebates. The rental costs for each family were lowered in proportion to the number of children. The loans and allowances were to be granted by the National Housing Loan Office and handled by the municipalities on the local level. The grants were intended primarily for towns and densely populated areas, but an additional paragraph later made it also possible to grant loans for housing in the countryside.[5] Families that consisted of three or more children less than sixteen years of age and one or both parents were regarded as "large" families. According to this definition, Swedish "large" families were the smallest in Europe. "Large" families in Italy had seven or more children, in Germany and France five or more and in Belgium four or more children.[6]

In June 1938 another act was issued to provide possibilities for large families with little means to build houses of their own.[7] The criterion for a large family here was the same as for the tenement houses, and the loans were handled by the same authorities.

Concern for housing had a long tradition in Swedish social debate. At the turn of the century the "housing problem" was even used as an equivalent of general social problems of the Swedish labour population. Yet, up to the 1930's housing was considered mainly a concern for private business or at the most

---

[3] *Ibid.*, p. 174.
[4] SFS 1935:512.
[5] SFS 1940:668.
[6] Cf. above footnote 1, and Glass 1940, p. 175.
[7] SFS 1938:247.

for the municipalities; only in periods of economic crisis was interference by the central government on a larger scale considered legitimate.[8] On the other hand, the building and construction industry was regarded as a particularly crucial area from the economic point of view. It was seen as especially suitable for investments during the general crisis of the 1930's. In 1930, when a temporary commitee on housing suggested governmental intervention in building and construction enterprises by the granting of loans or other credit, it was particularly stressed that the reasons for such intervention were not social but economic, meant to provide employment and to generally stimulate the Swedish economy.[9]

In 1933, however, following the Social Democratic take-over of political power, a Social Committee on Housing was appointed. Among the members of this committee were Alva and Gunnar Myrdal—an obvious link with the later constituted Committee on Population.[10] The task of the committee was to create a long-term programme for housing from a social policy perspective. It was to investigate the extent and conditions of slum dwellings in Swedish cities and towns and suggest appropriate measures to remedy or remove existing bad conditions in this sector. It was also to work on a short-term basis and propose measures to relieve the prevailing economic crisis. The work of the Social Committee on Housing was accompanied by two special housing censuses which revealed that bad housing conditions and especially overcrowding were very common in Sweden, somewhat to the surprise of the general Swedish public.[11]

The first substantial investigation and proposal of the committee was concerned with low income families with many children. It revealed bad, overcrowded housing conditions and suggested various means to better them. Step by step the original governmental interest in housing and construction had been qualified, first to encompass a specific social element and then, when large families were selected as the first important target by the Social Committee on Housing, a population policy element.

Population and housing problems were coupled together in yet another way. Gunnar Myrdal argued that with a declining population, investment activities would decline and the general economy would be adversely affected unless

---

[8] Outlines of Swedish housing policy are given by A. Myrdal 1941, pp. 232 ff. and Johansson 1962. Cf. also Holm 1976. — Evaluations of the scope and effects of Swedish housing policy during the 1930's differ. For critical opinions see Boberg et al. 1974 and Gustafsson 1974.

[9] Johansson 1962, pp. 567 ff.

[10] A. Myrdal 1941, pp. 220 ff., Johansson 1962, pp. 572 ff.

[11] Allmänna bostadsräkningen år 1933, (SOS 1936), Särskilda folkräkningen, 1935–36, part III, (SOS 1938). Cf. A. Myrdal 1944, p. 292.

109

special efforts were made to raise the general housing standard to a level that retained current demands for building and construction.[12]

Alva Myrdal later summed up the importance of housing for population policy in her book Nation and Family: "Higher housing standards are at least as necessary as higher nutritional standards. If houses are not healthy and homes not roomy, all attempts to raise the intellectual, moral, social and economic standards will to a large extent be ineffectual. When the existing housing standards ... are studied, certain crying evils stand out. Overcrowding for children is the worst of them." And further on in the same book she states that "a population policy would be meaningless without housing reforms".[13]

The *riksdag* accepted the reform to provide large, poor families with better housing suggested by the Social Committee on Housing. The decision was accompanied by a debate that did not deal with the problem of whether the measures should be approved or not, but rather which authority should control the financing and handling of it. Should it be handled by governmental and municipal authorities, or by private banking and building enterprises?[14] A couple of years later the same sort of discussion was held in the *riksdag* over the financial handling of the marriage loans. The Social Democratic aim to introduce a policy of greater public control of the economy here emerges clearly.[15] In both cases the importance of the debate was mainly one of principle, since the financial scope of both measures suggested was a comparatively moderate one.

Improved Housing for Large Families: Social Versus Population Policy Motives

Improved housing for large families was a reform created outside of (and before) the work in the Committee on Population. Its creation within the Social Committee on Housing also emphasises its undoubted social policy origin contrary to the two other measures treated in this context, both of which originated within the Committee on Population. But as already mentioned, population policy motives were strong in choosing the large families as the first target for the new social housing policy. Alva and Gunnar Myrdal's role as the connecting link in this respect has already been mentioned.[16]

[12] G. Myrdal 1940, pp. 152 ff.
[13] A. Myrdal 1941, p. 128. Cf. also *ibid.*, pp. 232 ff.
[14] Cervin 1974, pp. 12 ff.
[15] Cf. above ch. III.
[16] G. Myrdal also published a book together with U. Åhrén on social housing policy. G. Myrdal & U. Åhrén 1933.

Table 22. *Overcrowding in Sweden, by household type*

| | Per cent of dwelling with | | |
| | More than 1 $^1/_2$ persons per room | More than 2 persons per room | |
Household type	In urban districts	In urban districts	In rural districts
All households	34.5	12.6	12.3
Small households	7.1	0.2	–
Middle-sized households			
Without children	41.5	10.8	7.8
With children	48.9	5.4	4.7
Large households			
With 0–2 children	55.7	33.1	21.3
With 3 children or more	66.2	47.4	37.4

Sources: *Allmänna bostadsräkningen år 1933*, and *Särskilda folkräkningen 1935–1936*, III. From Alva Myrdal, Nation and Family, p. 247.

To what extent can the motives of social policy and population policy behind the measure be differentiated? As in the case of maternity relief such a differentiation becomes difficult since the main population policy aspect in this context was a qualitative one, as exemplified above in Alva Myrdal's statement. Closely linked to this discussion of the more general motives is the more concrete one of the policy's primary purpose. What were the direct aims of the policy? In what way was it to affect the large families? And finally, what did people in decision-making and influential positions know about the families in question?

In its report, the Committee on Social Housing gave its reasons for choosing the housing conditions of large, low income families as their first area of reform.[17] Overcrowding in urban areas was mentioned as the major social housing problem. This was mainly due to the fact that flats consisting of only one room and a kitchen were commonly used as family dwellings. Essentially, the problem of overcrowding was a children's problem; it was most common among families having more than two children. The recent, observed decreases in overcrowding was due to a substantial reduction in family size.

Children were thought to be particularly susceptible to the risk of mental and physical impairment caused by overcrowding. Measures aimed at doing

[17] SOU 1935: 2, pp. 1 ff.

away with overcrowding would therefore provide a more hygienic and morally healthier home environment for children.

If economic support is given, parents would also be able to have children without having to fear that bad housing conditions would harm their family —here a quantitative, pronatalist motive is discernible. Not least with regard to population policy considerations, the support should be provided in a way that could not be associated with poor relief or charity.[18] The wish to do away with the stigma attached to welfare which was prominent in connection with maternity relief is discernible here again. The report also stressed that the costs for children compete with those of housing; the more children a family has, the less it will be able to pay for housing. The reduction in rent should therefore be progressively related to the number of children of each family, and not to income.

So far the argument may be seen as simultaneously involving social policy and qualitative population policy. The population policy motives were, however, further developed. Housing policies were stated to be "a very important part of a positive population policy". The creation of better housing standards was seen as a "necessary prerequisite" for an increase of the marital birth rate. Overcrowding was also considered as one of the motives behind "extreme family limitation". In a summing-up, both qualitative and quantitative population policy aspects were stressed.[19]

Bad housing was thus considered as a major danger to the well-being, health and development of, in particular, children. This is wholly in line with the prominent place housing reform took in Swedish debate on social policy. The urgent social and population policy motives were linked together in the reasoning behind the measure in a way that makes it difficult to distinguish one from the other. However, they coincide as far as the population policy motives are of a quantitative nature, in the association of overcrowding with a decline in the number of children, and the notion that a good housing standard is a prerequisite for higher birth rates.

In some of the official comments made on the report by the government authorities, institutions and associations the pronatalist policy element is particularly stressed. According to the Swedish Medical Board, the current overcrowding to no small degree contributed to the "remarkable fall in fertility", a circumstance which should be considered as of "crucial importance" for the final decision on the matter.[20] A similar view was put forth by the leading Swedish women's society (*Fredrika Bremerförbundet*): further family limitation might well be the result of a continued insufficient supply of adequate housing

[18] *Ibid.*, pp. 47 ff.
[19] *Ibid.*, pp. 51 f.
[20] *Prop.* 1935:221, p. 11.

112

for families.[21] Population policy motives of a quantitative nature were also frequently mentioned in a general sort of way as constituting important grounds for recommending the measure.[22] The danger of physical and mental impairment to children as a result of overcrowding was also often mentioned by those favourably disposed to the reform.[23] Despite the favourable attitude in principle to improvement of housing conditions for large, low income families, there was, however, also criticism in the official comments, in two motions submitted to the *riksdag* on the matter, and in the *riksdag* debate.[24]

This criticism centered around the fact that the building of special tenement houses for large families—even if they could be mixed with other families —would create *segregational* housing, which might have a negative impact. The houses might be considered as houses for the poor with the usual welfare and poor relief stigma attached to them. The assembling of people in the same limited area that were both economically weak and had many children could create undesirable consequences for the children. "If the population policy goal is to be attained, help should be given as discreetly as possible."[25]

The argument over segregational housing recurred also after a decision had been reached on the measure, and the problem was again debated when an investigation of housing for large families was carried out by the Social Board in 1941.[26] The argument undoubtedly contributed to the abolition of the measure in 1948. This problem is important from the "porpose-effect" point of view. It will, therefore, be considered again in the following in-depth study of people living in large family tenements.

Implementation: Quantitative Aspects

About 20 000 large families were in need of flats in the planned tenement houses according to the report of the Committee on Social Housing.[27] In his proposal to the *riksdag* on the matter in 1935 the Minister of Social Affairs

[21] *Ibid.*, p. 13.

[22] *Ibid.*, pp. 11 ff.

[23] *Ibid.*, *passim*.

[24] MFK 1935: 332, MAK 1935: 572, pp. 11 ff., FK 1935: 38 and AK 1935: 41.

[25] MFK 1935: 332, p. 3.

[26] *Socialstyrelsens undersökning rörande bostäder för mindre bemedlade barnrika familjer.* (Unprinted report in *Konseljakter*, 1950, February 17th, *Socialdepartementet*, National Archives, Stockholm; in abbreviated form printed in *Sociala Meddelanden*, 1942, 11.) The remaining primary material from the investigation is located in the archive of *Socialstyrelsens 5:e byrå: Bostäder för barnrika familjer, sign. H II bm*, Archives of the Central Bureau of Statistics, Stockholm.

[27] SOU 1935: 2. — It might be worth mentioning that the so-called Committee on Retrenchment in 1942, when dealing with housing for large families estimated the need at 50 000 flats (*P.M. angående lån och bidrag av statsmedel för beredande av hyresbostäder åt mindre bemedlade barnrika familjer.* Unprinted report in *Kommitté* 864: 29, National Archives, Stockholm.)

Table 23. *Families living in tenement houses for large families and receiving rent rebates, 1935–1948. Fiscal years*

Year	Number of families
1935/36	1 390
1936/37	2 603
1937/38	3 622
1938/39	4 681
1939/40	5 727
1940/41	5 807
1941/42	6 211
1942/43	7 178
1943/44	7 990
1944/45	9 382
1945/46	10 149
1946/47	10 781
1947/48	12 124

Source: *Berättelse över Statens byggnadslånebyrås verksamhet under budgetåret 1947/48*, p. 22.

reiterated this approximation of the need. A three-year programme meant for the building of 20 000 flats was suggested.[28] But the proposed grant of thirty million Sw. crowns for the first fiscal year was drastically cut by the *riksdag* to only ten millions.[29]

It is not clear whether or not this cut directly affected the outcome of the reform which fell far short of its original goal. As shown in Table 23, the original goal had not even been reached 13 years later in 1948 when the institution of special tenement houses for large families was done away with and replaced by general housing allowances for families in need.[30]

This holds true even when the one-family houses built according to the ordinance of 1938 are taken into consideration.[31] As could be expected, the majority of the tenement houses were built in towns, whereas the one-family houses were built in the countryside. Tenement houses were, moreover, concentrated to the southern and central parts of Sweden, but the one-family

[28] *Prop.* 1935:221.
[29] RS 1935:344. — The cut was proposed by the parliamentary committee handling the proposal, and Ulf Cervin, in his analysis of the treatment of the proposal by the *riksdag*, suggests that the cut might have been the result of a compromise between members of the Social Democratic and Agrarian parties. (Cervin 1974, p. 12.)
[30] On this decision, see Johansson 1962.
[31] *Berättelse över Statens byggnadslånebyrås verksamhet under budgetåret* 1947/48, Table 4.

Map 6. Houses for large families. One-family houses 1939–40.

Source: Socialstyrelsens femte byrå: Bostäderna för barnrika familjer, (SCB).

houses were found throughout the country (Maps 6 and 7). This is surprising since fertility was higher and large families were more numerous in the northern parts of Sweden. On the other hand, most of the population there lived in rural areas.

The implementation of the reform for improved housing for large families, at least quantitatively, was not entirely successful. The cut in the initial grant has already been mentioned as a possible cause of this. Of far greater importance, however, was the role of the local authorities. In an important respect the subsidising of housing for large families differed from both marriage loans and maternity relief. These two reforms were uniformly applied throughout the

115

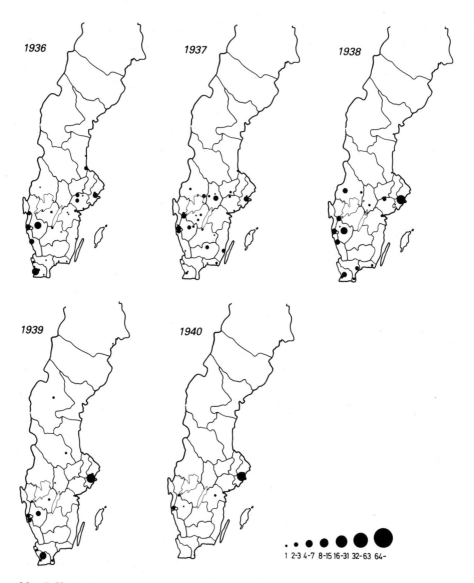

Map 7. Houses for large families. Tenement houses built 1936–40.
Source: Socialstyrelsens femte byrå: Bostäderna för barnrika familjer, (SCB).

country—any individual or family could apply for them and would, at least in principle, follow a similar procedure and be judged in the same manner. This was also true for large families wanting to build homes of their own using the advantages provided by the ordinance of 1938. But in the case of the tenement houses for large families, the towns and municipalities played a crucial role in deciding whether the houses were to be built or not, and accordingly whether large families in need of better housing would be given the possibility of obtaining that housing. Although the National Housing Loan Office provided loans for one half or more of the amount needed for each building scheme, the towns had to provide free building space, to supply extra loans if needed and to cover any losses caused by the tenants' inability to pay their rent.[32] On the other hand, the rent rebates were wholly provided by the state.

After they were built, the houses were to be administered either by the towns directly or by so-called *allmännyttiga bostadsföretag*—mostly cooperatively owned non-profit housing companies—the most prominent of which belonged to the National Association of Tenants' Savings and Building Society. In practice these companies also initiated the building of tenement houses for large families. Although the incentives were strong, the decision for the implementation of the reform thus lay with the towns and municipalities which had to make certain investments and take certain responsibilities.

The political situation in the towns may have had an influence here. It seems probable, for instance, that towns with a Social Democratic majority would have been more prone to take advantage of the reform than those with other parties in power. Ulf Cervin has touched upon this problem in an essay on the housing reform for large families. In 1938 the socialist parties (Social Democrats and Communists) held a majority in about half of the 114 Swedish towns. Up to March 1938, tenement houses for large families were built or under construction in 51 towns (45 per cent); 32 of these had a socialist majority (63 per cent), in 15 (29 per cent) the Conservatives and the Liberal party held a joint majority and in four towns (8 per cent) the political representation was equally divided between the socialists and others.

The building of tenement houses seems therefore to have been more attractive in towns with a socialist majority. But Cervin means that too far-reaching conclusions should not be drawn from this fact.[33] One might add that the *need* for housing of this kind probably was greater in towns with a large labour population, towns that by this very circumstance were also more likely to be governed by a socialist majority. Both political and practical reasons may thus have played a role for whether tenement houses for large families were built or not. Nevertheless, it is obvious that the reform for improved housing for large families did not receive universal acceptance—in many places only a few such houses were built.[34]

[32] SFS 1935:512.

[33] Cervin 1974, p. 21.

[34] In only six places did the number of flats in tenement houses for large families exceed one hundred in 1942. On the other hand in 23 places there were less than ten such flats. (*P.M. angående lån och bidrag, etc., Kommitté* 864:29, National Archives, Stockholm.)

Implementation: Qualitative Aspects

So far only the quantitative aspects of the implementation have been treated. Although the measure was a comparative failure quantitatively, this does not render the study of effects on those families who did benefit from the reform less interesting. In this context qualitative aspects are also of importance. Did the tenement houses provide improved standards in comparison to previous housing of the families concerned? How did this kind of housing compare with other tenement houses built during the same period? What did the families themselves think of their new housing standards? And what was the influence, so much discussed in the debate preceding the reform, of separate housing on large families?

In 1941 the Social Board conducted an investigation of the tenement houses and one-family houses for large families.[35] As shown in Table 24, the greater part of the families, particularly those living in the three largest cities, had a larger number of rooms. Their standard had also improved in other respects. Central heating, bathrooms and communal washing machines were new conveniences for most of them. Moreover, the rent rebates actually compared to their previous situation meant a decrease in rental costs for many of the families. The one-family houses also represented an increase in both space and rooms for the families concerned.

The investigation of the Social Board showed that the houses for large families represented an increase in space and an improvement in other housing facilities for the families moving into them. But how did they compare with other tenement houses built at the same time? Such a comparison can be made by using an unprinted report from the so-called Committee on Retrenchment which, during the war, prepared plans for diminishing public expenses in different sectors.

In its investigation, made in 1942, the committee found that the standard of the tenement houses for large families was lower than that of other similar houses built at the same time.[36] For example, generally cheaper materials were used for floors and decoration, none of the flats had refrigerators, and so forth. Living space in tenement houses for large families was also more limited than in other flats containing the same number of rooms.[37] Similar differences in standard were assumed to exist between the one-family houses for large families and similar one-family houses.

On the one hand, the special houses for large families represented an improvement both as to living space and standard compared to the previous

---

[35] *Socialstyrelsens undersökning rörande bostäder för mindre bemedlade barnrika familjer.*

[36] *P.M. angående lån och bidrag etc. Komm.* 864:29, (National Archives, Stockholm.)

[37] Cf. the in-depth study of tenement houses for large families in Borås, p. 121 ff.

Table 24. *Number of rooms for families in tenement houses compared to previous housing.*
1941

	More	Per cent	Un- changed	Per cent	Less	Per cent
Stockholm	1 256	76.0	367	22.2	30	1.8
Gothenburg	1 399	86.8	202	12.5	11	0.7
Malmö	147	79.5	38	20.5	–	–
Towns with 30 000– 100 000 inhabitants	458	70.9	180	27.9	8	1.2
Towns with 10 000– 30 000 inhabitants	270	57.0	176	37.1	28	5.9
Towns with less than 10 000 inhabitants	51	71.8	18	25.4	2	2.8

Source: Socialstyrelsens undersökning rörande bostäder för mindre bemedlade barnrika familjer. (Sociala Meddelanden, 1942, 11.)

housing conditions for the families concerned, but on the other hand they did not offer the same standard as other similarly built houses during the same period.

Experiences and Opinions of Tenement Houses for Large Families

What did the people themselves think of their new homes? The investigation of the Social Board provides access to some contemporary information on this matter. Besides asking the families themselves, the Social Board also turned to other people, social workers, teachers, municipal officials and persons renting flats in the tenement houses without fulfilling the requirements for rent rebates for their opinions on such housing.[38] The information was obtained by means of standardised questionnaires and did not therefore permit much in the way of individually expressed opinions. Answers were obtained from more than sixty per cent of all families living in such houses and receiving rent rebates in September 1941. Families who had lived less than six months in the houses were not questioned. This part of the investigation was probably to some extent instigated by the current assumption and fear of unfavourable social and other consequences resulting from the kind of separate housing created by the tenement houses for large families.

[38] *Socialstyrelsens undersökning rörande bostäder för mindre bemedlade barnrika familjer.*

As already mentioned, moving into these houses meant an improvement both with regard to the number of rooms and other facilities for the overwhelming majority of the families. They were obviously also well aware of this and were satisfied with this improvement. Little dissatisfaction is found among the answers to the questionnaire. Slightly more than 20 per cent were not satisfied with the kitchen equipment, but more than 85 per cent expressed their satisfaction with the communal laundry facilities and machines. There was some criticism of the number and size of the cupboards, wardrobes, food-cellars, etc.

The children naturally received special attention in the report. It was found that the care of infants and small children had become easier and that hygienic and other conditions were better. Children of school age were found to have had better opportunities for doing their homework undisturbed. Although two-thirds of the families stated that they would prefer houses of their own, if possible, the total impression was very favourable. But it was pointed out in the report that many persons might have hesitated to answer negatively or voice criticism to an official authority such as the Social Board. Moreover, the questionnaires were distributed and collected by the respective house managements, a fact which might also have restrained criticism.

Other statements, though voiced somewhat later, corroborated this positive picture. People, who had lived in flats for large families expressed their general satisfaction with the improvement in housing standard and their enjoyment of such items as having more than one room, a bathroom of their own and hot running water.[39]

Similar positive judgements were found among the answers by social workers, teachers, etc. to the questionnaires of the Social Board.[40] Many of these individuals believed that hygiene and health among children had improved, although there were some warnings about the risk of epidemics. They also thought that the better standard of housing and household equipment facilitated the woman's work in the home. But in their answers these respondents also mentioned certain negative consequences of tenement housing for large families—gangs were easily formed among the more grown-up children which might foster asocial tendencies, and make it more difficult for parents to maintain their authority. Here the problem of separate housing for large families comes to the fore.

Both the families and the other respondents were asked whether any drawbacks or disadvantages resulted from separate housing. Seventeen per cent of

[39] Cederström-Friman *et al.* 1979, pp. 174 ff. — Interview with Mrs. Annie Andersson, Gothenburg, a former resident in a tenement house for large families. Interview with a former social worker in Borås.

[40] *Socialstyrelsens undersökning rörande bostäder för mindre bemedlade barnrika familjer.*

the families answered this question in the affirmative; this answer was more common among respondents living in the large complexes of tenements. As already mentioned, the formation of gangs, lack of authority etc. were thought of as undesirable outcomes of separate housing for large families by the other respondents. Again, larger complexes of tenement houses were more frequently pointed out than others. On the other hand, complaints of criminality were very scarce. There was also a recurring notion that some kind of social stigma was attached to those living in houses for large families. Both parents and children were treated contemptuously, and the houses and families living in them were given such names as "rabbit hutches" and "myrdalings", the last of which testifies to an awareness of the Myrdals' role in this context. One of the respondents suggested that the reason for such behaviour was a traditional contempt for people living on welfare and poor relief.[41] It should be pointed out, however, that many people, both among the families and the other respondents, denied that such negative attitudes or treatment were common or even existed.

The investigation of the Social Board and other evidence point in two directions. On one hand, the houses for large families seemed to have meant both a quantitative and a qualitative improvement to the families concerned. On the other hand, the assembling of many children in a relatively confined area and the attitudes and behaviour of the surrounding society were perceived as negative consequences of such separate housing.

Improved Housing for Large Families: An In-depth Study of 192 Families

The investigation of the Social Board provided some contemporary comments and views on special housing for large families. But a more in-depth study of the impact of the reform also requires an investigation of the actual behaviour of the families to determine their family patterns.

Borås, a medium-sized town in the southwestern part of Sweden was chosen as suitable for this purpose. The town had 48 000 inhabitants in 1940 and was dominated industrially by textile factories which traditionally provided work for whole families; women, men and in earlier years also children.[42] The number of large families was unusually high in Borås and the town was growing with surpluses of both births and in-migrants. (Se Table 25.) Furthermore, the town contained a large labour population and was governed by a

[41] Interview with Mrs. Annie Andersson, Gothenburg. Cf. Dahlström 1951.
[42] On Borås generally see Östling 1949 and Dungel 1976. On the textile industry in Borås, see Friberg 1969, Persson 1942 and *Borås Wäfveri Aktiebolag* 1870–1945.

121

Table 25. *Births, deaths, in-migrants, out-migrants and total population in Borås, 1933–1942.*

Year	Births	Deaths	In-migrants	Out-migrants	Total population
1933	560	370	2 109	1 444	40 656
1934	604	355	2 696	1 627	42 021
1935	707	375	2 880	1 823	43 365
1936	708	375	3 255	1 950	45 039
1937	753	403	3 211	2 434	46 178
1938	769	415	3 010	2 495	47 061
1939	850	391	6 337	5 839	47 931
1940	823	370	5 090	5 167	48 328
1941	870	422	4 631	4 603	48 873
1942	907	361	4 140	4 116	49 421

Source: *SOS: Befolkningsrörelsen*, 1933–1942, Tab. 3 and 4.

socialist majority. It is not surprising then that the municipal board reacted favourably to both the proposal of the Committee on Social Housing and later the official ordinance.[43] The town thus became one of the first to build special houses for large families.[44] It did so on a comparatively large scale.

Three different building and housing companies (the most important of which was to become the local branch of the Tenants' Savings and Building Society) rapidly engaged in building houses for large families. One of these, the cooperatively organised *AB Egna Hem* specialised in the construction of small, privately owned houses. It contrived to use the financial advantage offered by the central government to build a number of one-family houses which could be rented to large families on the same conditions as flats in the tenements. When their children had grown up and the families were no longer entitled to rent rebates, they could buy these houses.[45] By helping themselves in the building of the houses, families also could obtain a lower price when they later bought it. It is therefore not surprising that carpenters, painters and masons were

[43] Some suspicions were, however, voiced as to the possible dangers of concentrating too many large families in one place. *Borås kommunalblad* 1935: 2, 1935: 10.

[44] According to one source, Gunnar Myrdal was personally responsible in urging the building of special houses for large families in Borås. Dyring 1944, pp. 34 ff. and p. 53, where the author says that "we all but promised Myrdal to start building houses for large families". Cf. also *Sociala Meddelanden* 1938: 12, pp. 822 f.

[45] Minutes in the archive of *AB Egna Hem* in Borås (Borås Municipal Archives), *AB Egna Hem i Borås,* esp. pp. 24 ff.

among the more frequent tenants.[46] Of the 37 such families specially investigated no less than 31 later bought their houses, indicating a very low rate of migration among these families. On average thirteen years passed between the family moving into the house and their purchasing it.

The other two companies built tenement houses. The standard of these seems to have been about the same as for similar houses built during the same period. In their early years of construction one of the companies, *AB Barnbostäder*, however, provided lavatories instead of bathrooms for each separate flat. Bathrooms for communal use were installed in the basements. The tenements were usually three storey buildings with flats of two or three rooms. The total area of each flat was rather small. In the houses built by the Tenants' Savings and Building Society which have been especially looked into in this context the total area for two-room flats was 44 square meters, and for three-room flats 53 square meters.[47] Other services were also provided, such as the already-mentioned communal laundry facilities and a combined day-care centre and kindergarten built adjacent to the houses. According to the statistics provided in the annual reports, these were frequently attended. Also school-children could spend their afternoons there, if the parents were working.[48] Clubs and courses of various kinds were provided for the young people among the residents. There they were able to learn sewing, cooking, drawing and carpentry and could join in such activities as singing, sports, table tennis, etc.

The local press regularly reported on the building of these new houses for large families in a positive vein. In a newspaper article from 1941 the houses were described and praised; the children were said to be "nice and well-behaved, and good at helping their parents with smaller sisters and brothers". The courses and clubs were also favourably mentioned.[49] But also critics were to be found. One of the local politicians, for example, warned that the segregated environment might create criminal gangs among the youth.[50]

The housing supply in Borås was described as insufficient but improving during the last five years of the 1930's. During the war, however, building did not keep up with the demand and a housing shortage was reported.[51]

---

[46] *Socialstyrelsens 5:e byrå: Bostäder för barnrika familjer* (Archives of the Central Bureau of Statistics, Stockholm).

[47] *Borås kommunalblad* 1935: 12, 1936: 10. — Descriptions of flats in the archive of HSB, Borås. — More information on the history and activities of HSB (The Tenants' Savings and Building Societies) is given in Svensson 1976 and Lundewall 1976.

[48] Annual reports, archive of HSB, Borås. The high rate of employment in the textile factories outside the home among women created a special demand for day-care centers. Some of these were provided by the employers. Cf. *Borås Wäfveri Aktiebolag*, p. 36.

[49] *Borås kommunalblad* 1942: 10.

[50] *Svenska Stadsförbundets tidskrift* 1943: 4 (cited in Cervin 1974).

[51] *Borås kommunalblad* 1935: 10, 1936: 11, 1937: 7, 1939: 7, 1943: 1 and 1945: 5.

Method and Population

The documents from the investigation of the Social Board contain information on all families living in tenement houses for large families in September 1941. From these sources, information on the 192 families then living in special houses for large families in Borås was excerpted, and the families were afterwards identified in the local population registers and other records of the two parishes in Borås. The families were then traced in the population registers both backwards and forwards in time—backwards to the date of the parents' marriage and forwards to 1952.[52] Information was obtained on date and place of birth, marriage, children and on all migrations of the family in or outside Borås during the period in question; men's occupations were also recorded, but unfortunately data on women's occupations were only irregularly given in the registers, and were therefore unusable.

The inhabitants of two residential blocks, occupied by workers and their families and not containing special housing for large families, were chosen as a suitable control group. One of these blocks was owned by a textile factory and accordingly almost exclusively rented to textile workers; the other contained a more "mixed" population. Information on these groups was excerpted from the enumerative lists of the Swedish population census of 1940.[53] In contrast to the houses for large families, flats in these residential blocks were rented to both families and single persons. For the present purposes, couples with children are the most important group; single parents with children, childless couples and single persons are therefore omitted.

The control group consisted of 104 families. Data on date and place of birth, date of marriage, number of children and husband's occupation were collected for each of these families in 1940. The total amount of information obtained on the control group was more limited than that collected for the group of large families. This limitation was partly due to the considerable amount of time and work involved in tracing people through the population registers of several parishes. The fact that, with regard to an essential feature of the investigation, the migrational pattern, the large families themselves functioned as a "control group" made the collection of information on migration for the control group unnecessary. Migrations before and after moving into the houses for large families were instead compared.

[52] *Socialstyrelsens 5:e byrå: Bostäder för barnrika familjer.* (Archives of the Central Bureau of Statistics, Stockholm.) General population registers, birth records, marriage records, records of in- and out-migration in the parish archives of *Borås Caroli, Borås Gustaf Adolf* and of 58 other parishes. (Cf. bibliography.)

[53] The population census of 1940. Extracts from the local population registers. (Archives of the Central Bureau of Statistics, Stockholm.) Dates of marriage were not recorded in these lists but were available in the local population records in Borås.

Houses for Large Families—Improvement but Also Segregation?

The large families in Borås fall into two categories: those who lived in tenement houses and those who rented one-family houses. Over seventy per cent (140) lived in tenement houses; most of them (113) in tenements built by the Tenants' Savings and Building Society. The rest (51) rented one-family houses. But since all one-family houses were built in the same area, both forms resulted in segregated housing.

Both categories, of course, differed from families in general in having more than the average number of children. But they differed in yet another way. They lived in buildings whose residents were made up solely of large families. The 104 families of the control group on the other hand lived together with a mixture of people—101 single persons, 31 single parents with children and 22 childless couples. Several of the single persons were probably lodgers. The tenants in the special houses for large families were not allowed to have lodgers, since it would counteract the very purpose of creating more room.[54]

In Borås—as elsewhere—the normal flats for labourers consisted of one room and a kitchen. According to a contemporary report, the families usually lived and slept in the kitchen, thereby keeping the other room in nice and presentable order.[55] Thus, for the large families, although they might still be crowded, the new flats meant an improvement with regard to number of rooms, compared to their previous situation. This was true for 150, or 78 per cent of the families. The generally higher standard of the new houses also undoubtedly meant an important improvement. The families in Borås who were able to rent houses or flats especially built for large families thus experienced better housing conditions but at the price of being segregated.

The Large Families in Borås: Social Characteristics

What were the social and demographic characteristics of the 192 large families in Borås? By definition their economic conditions were comparatively poor; they also had at least three children. Socially most of them belonged to a lower working-class stratum. In 72 families (37.5 per cent) the fathers were textile workers, in 57 (30 per cent) they were unskilled workers of other kinds, in 12 (6 per cent) they were employed in office work or a similar occupation, in 42 they were skilled workers and artisans (22 per cent) and in 9 (4.5 per cent) they had shops of their own or were industrial foremen, etc. Women were often recorded

---

[54] SFS 1935: 512 § 19. — Special permission to have lodgers could be obtained. Cf. Minutes of the Tenants' Savings and Building Society in Borås (HSB archives, Borås) and Minutes of *AB Egna Hem*, Borås (Municipal archives, Borås).
[55] *Borås kommunalblad* 1935: 10.

as textile workers—mostly seamstresses. As mentioned above, carpenters, painters, masons, etc. were particularly numerous among the families renting one-family houses.

Socially, the large families in Borås are more comparable to those who received maternity relief than to those who received marriage loans. However, there were differences between the large families living in tenement houses and those living in one-family houses. The latter attracted special occupational categories and possibly also a certain personality type, one which retained such attributes as saving and long-term planning (also with regard to family size). Accordingly, in the following, families living in tenements and families living in one-family houses will be treated separately when necessary.

The Large Families: Women's Age at Marriage

Both the maternity relief receivers and the women in the marriage loan sample were younger at marriage than the average marrying population. Not unexpectedly, this was true also of the mothers in the large families. Their mean age at marriage was 23 years and 9 months; with a median of 23 years and 6 months. These figures should be compared to 26.3 and 26.0 for the country as a whole.[56]

Divorces were rare among the large families—only nine or 4.5 per cent of the families ended in divorce before the women reached 46 years of age. An additional couple of cases separated without formal divorce. Since childless marriages end in divorce far more often than marriages with children, the fact that these families had many children may explain their stability.[57] An additional factor here might be the poor economic situation of these families; divorce was probably something they could not easily afford. Since the probability of divorce diminishes proportionally to the duration of the marriage, the fact that these families had been married for some time might also partially explain the low divorce rate. Still, the high cohesion among these families contradicts those theories which presuppose a general instability of marriage among large and poor families.[58]

Death was a more common cause of the dissolution of a marriage. 19 or nearly ten per cent of the marriages ended with the death of the husband or wife before the woman was 46 years old—a higher rate than for the marriage loan sample and a fact that probably indicates generally poorer living conditions.

[56] *SOS: Folkmängden och dess förändringar 1966.* Table 3:7. Mean, median and quartile age at first marriages and remarriages of husband and wife.
[57] See e.g., Cherlin 1977.
[58] Cf. Askham 1975, pp. 2 ff.

Table 26. *The large families in Borås: Women's age at marriage. Complete marriages, and marriages dissolved by divorce or death. Mean and median values*

	Number	Mean age at marriage	Median age at marriage
Complete marriages	164	24 years 2 months	23 years 6 months
Divorces	9	21 years 11 months	21 years 6 months
Deaths	19	22 years 6 months	22 years 5 months

As with the women in the marriage loan group, age at marriage has been calculated with regard to whether the marriage was later dissolved by death or by divorce. Women in marriages dissolved by death married at a somewhat younger age than women in complete marriages. Women whose marriages were disrupted by divorce also married at younger ages, about two years younger. This was comparable to the divorced women in the marriage loan sample. The number of cases of divorce are, however, too few to allow any reliable comparisons (Table 26).

The Large Families: Family Size and Fertility

The families had to be "large" in order to be able to benefit from the reform. That is, they had to consist of parents and at least three children under 16 years of age. But how "large" were the families in Borås?

On average there were 4.8 children per family. The total number of children was 922. 98 were either children from earlier marriages and/or extra-marital children, many of whom were born to parents who later married. If these last two categories are excluded, an average of 4.3 children were born per marriage.

Which families had the most children to care for—those living in tenement houses or those living in one-family houses? The 140 families in the tenement flats had, on average, 4.7 children; the 52 in the one-family houses had 5.0 children. The difference is slight and family size can therefore be said to have been about the same in both types of housing.

When comparing the family size of the large families and the families in the control group, it must be remembered that the information for the control group was taken from cross-sectional census data and therefore only indicates family size at a specific point in time. At least some of these families would probably have had more children. To avoid losses of information due to children moving away from home only families with parents married after 1925 are considered. Family size among these 48 families was, on average, 1.7 in

Table 27. *Family pattern of the large families in Borås. Number of children per family in marriages which lasted until the woman was 46 years or more. Complete marriages*

Number of children	Number of families	Per cent
1	2	1.2
2	12	7.5
3	36	22.5
4	42	26.2
5	31	19.4
6	18	11.3
7	11	6.9
8	7	4.4
9	–	–
10	1	0.6
Total	160[a]	100

[a] Four families, in which the woman was over 34 years old at the time of marriage, have been omitted here.

1940. When differentiated into two groups, one consisting of marriages contracted 1925–31, the other of marriages contracted after 1931, the average number of children is 2.0 for the first group and 1.5 for the second. The first figure indicates completed or nearly completed family size among the control group.

The distribution of marriages according to the number of children is given in Table 27 for the large families. The figures are for complete marriages only. Children born before the actual marriage ceremony are not included, which explains the presence in the table of families with only one or two children.

Families with four children were most common, though families with both three and five children were also common. 46 families or 28.8 per cent had more than five children. In the control group two children was the usual number in the marriages contracted before 1932; one child was most frequent among those married after 1931. None of these families had more than four children in 1940.

Total marital fertility by age at marriage is presented in Table 28 as the number of children in relation to the number of woman-years in marriage. The figures for complete marriages are given separately.

Table 28 allows comparisons to be made with the marriage loan sample, where the corresponding figures are: 114.5 (15–19 years of age), 98.8 (20–24), 91.1 (25–29) and 87.7 (30–34). The fertility of the large families is considerably higher, regardless of the age at marriage. Even among those married after the

Table 28. *The large families in Borås: Total marital fertility by age at marriage. Number of children per thousand woman-years in marriage*

Age at marriage	15–19	20–24	25–29	30–34	35–39
All marriages	173.1	217.2	233.9	260.7	186.0
Complete marriages only	167.4	211.0	230.2	260.7	186.0

age of 34, fertility was as high as two children per ten years of marriage. An interesting difference in comparison with the marriage loan sample is, that instead of fertility being highest among those who married young, it is highest among women who married between 30–34 years of age.

It must be remembered that Table 28 gives the number of children in relation to time in marriage. Those in the group who were older at marriage thus had relatively more children per year in marriage than those who were younger. In contrast, those who were younger and accordingly had a longer time in marriage also had *more* children, but show a somewhat lower fertility per year in marriage.

Table 29 gives the mean number of children by age at marriage. Marital fertility is given by age at childbirth and by duration of marriage in Table 30. Fertility was particularly high during the first five years of marriage, even among those women who married comparatively late. Although fertility on the whole decreased in relation to the time in marriage, there are a couple of instances where it was higher during the third five-yearperiod than during the second.

In contrast to the marriage loan sample, where fertility was very low after the first ten years of marriage, it continued to remain high among the 192 large

Table 29. *The large families in Borås: Mean number of children by women's age at marriage*

	Age at marriage					
	15–19	20–24	25–29	30–34	35–39	All
Mean number of children for all families	4.96	4.55	4.15	3.10	1.50	4.3
Number of marriages	27	103	48	10	4	192
Mean number of children for complete marriages	4.33	4.75	4.15	3.10	1.50	4.4
Number of marriages	24	81	45	10	4	164

Table 30. *The large families: Marital fertility as number of children per thousand woman-years in marriage: By age and duration of marriage*

Age at marriage	Duration of marriage in years						
	0–4	5–9	10–14	15–19	20–24	25–29	All
15–19	754.9						754.9
20–24	493.5	238.4					477.6
25–29	440.6	218.4	238.4				330.0
30–34	353.8	222.5	175.6	–			212.4
35–39	425.2	221.0	161.7	58.5	85.1		139.5
40–44	114.3	25.1	94.7	48.3	22.2	–	42.6
All	456.6	212.7	161.6	51.4	26.6	–	214.1

families. Not only was fertility generally higher among the large families, it also showed a somewhat inconsistent pattern which indicates irregular family limitation. Of course, one must not exclude the possibility that some of the parents planned for a comparatively large family, but given the general economic and social circumstances of these families, it seems more likely that most of the children were neither planned nor regularly avoided. Interviews with members of these families, though conducted much later, suggest that this was true. For example, one informant recalled that: "I did not want more children, but I was happy when they were born."[59] One must also remember that nearly a fourth of the families had only three children which in turn indicates successful efforts at family limitation.[60]

Premaritally Born and Conceived Children as Indicators of Non-planning

In previous chapters it has been assumed that attitudes and behaviour with regard to fertility reflect and are part of more general attitudes and perceptions of desired goals in life and the ability to reach them. The families in the marriage loan sample showed a pattern of fertility that indicated ambition and ability to control and plan their lives in a long-term perspective, including the planning of a family according to a strict pattern of family limitation. For the

[59] Interview with Mrs. Annie Andersson, Gothenburg.

[60] Lee Rainwater, in his study of the connection between poverty and large families, suggests that a lack of family planning and of regular efforts at family limitation are most common among families with very traditional sex role patterns, where consequently, the wife has little to say on family matters. Unfortunately, we cannot ascertain whether this is true also here. Rainwater 1960.

Table 31. *The large families in Borås: Number of families with premaritally born or conceived children (completed marriages),[a] compared with control group*

	Pre-maritally born children	Per cent	Pre-maritally conceived children	Per cent	Others	Per cent	Total
Large families	55	33.5	82	50	27	16.5	164
Control group	8	17	22	46	18	37	48

[a] Women who already had children and were expecting when they married are only included among those who had premaritally born children.

recipients of maternity relief, a less planned family pattern was observed in a context of comparable poverty associated with a sense of helplessness and a short-term planning perspective.

In the case of the recipients of maternity relief it was suggested that, in this context, the rates of premaritally born or conceived children might be used to predict later attitudes and behaviour with regard to fertility. However, as was pointed out earlier, these factors might also be a reflection of attitudes towards marriage, attitudes which may have differed among different social groups. Among the maternity relief group, the share of families with children born or conceived before marriage was higher compared to the higher social strata and compared to socially and economically similar groups. Against the background of these results, a high rate of both premaritally born and premaritally conceived children ought to be found among the large families in Borås (Table 31).

As much as 83.5 per cent of the women in the large families had or were expecting children at marriage. The corresponding figure for the control group is lower, 62 per cent, though this is also very high. Half of the women in the large families were expecting when they married. In the control group 46 per cent were expecting which was exactly the same as for those receiving maternity relief. Among the large families 33.5 per cent of the women had premaritally born children. In the marriage loan group premarital conceptions were less common (23.5 per cent) and the number of marriages with premaritally born children was as low as 5.3 per cent. The marriage loan sample, however, also contained childless marriages, a fact which might partially explain the lower figures. But even so the differences are considerable.

In the case of the maternity relief group it was observed that children born or conceived before marriage (a phenomenon that was all but non-existent among the higher social strata) seemed to be a part of a general working-class pattern of marriage. Similar attitudes and behaviour with regard to sexual intercourse before marriage have been observed among the growing landless proletariat during the 19th century, and can in an historical perspective also be linked to the traditionally weak position of the marriage ceremony in the Scandinavian countries.[61]

The large families in Borås displayed typical characteristics of a working class marriage and family pattern. But as in the case of the maternity relief group, there were differences within the same social stratum, differences which in both cases point in the same direction. Low ages at marriage and high rates of premaritally born or conceived children resulted in, on the average, many children. Again these characteristics served as predictors of a less planned over-all pattern of life and consequently also of larger families.

In an essay on individual time horizons Birgitta Odén defines a planning horizon as the time perspective that is related to individually perceived possibilities to act—it follows that the greater such possibilities are, the longer planning horizons will tend to be and vice versa.[62] Applied to the large families considered here, this would mean that limited resources result in a sense of helplessness and accordingly in short planning horizons. As in the case of the maternity relief group, a comparative lack of regular family limitation is to be expected. Again, people having the least resources and conforming least to the general economic rationality of the surrounding society are precisely the ones that fulfill the reproductive goals of this very society.

Special Housing for Large Families: Persistence Rates as Measures of Acceptance

What in reality did the new flats and houses mean to the 192 families? In part this question has already been answered. In the above-mentioned investigation by the Social Board, most reactions to the reform were positive. Since, as was pointed out above, the report may have been biased, more evidence is needed. By examining the actual behaviour of the families before and after moving into the new housing facilities, it should be possible to determine whether or not they were satisfied with their new situation. One means of doing this is to examine persistence rates. Did these families move often before coming to their

---

[61] On marriage in Sweden in an historical perspective, see L. Carlsson 1969 and Kälvemark 1978. On premarital conceptions in different social strata and in their relation to marriage, see Eriksson–Rogers 1978, pp. 117 ff., Kälvemark 1977: 3 and 1980, Löfgren 1969 and Winberg 1975, pp. 217 ff. This development of a specific working-class pattern of marriage may also be an important part of the recent trend towards cohabitation without marriage in Sweden. Cf. Lewin 1979.

[62] Odén 1975, pp. 108 f.

new homes? Afterwards, did they often change residence or did they stay for long periods in the same place?

To answer these questions every change of residence has been recorded for each family starting at the marriage of the parents and continuing until 1952. This means that the families were followed in the records for a period of eleven to fifteen years after their move into the large family houses (the first families moved in in 1936).[63] On average, each family moved six times before coming to the houses for large families. Their average time in marriage was 7.7 years. When time is standardised by putting number of migrations in relation to number of years in marriage the resulting figure is 779, or nearly eight migrations during a ten-year-period. In other words, the families moved on average nearly once a year.

This is a very high rate of migration. It can be compared to the extraordinarily high migration rates of the landless labourers (called *statare*) and their families that during the 19th and early 20th centuries were known in Sweden for their poverty, their large families and their numerous migrations. Since they were also similar in other respects to the families considered here, it might be worth mentioning that Ingrid Eriksson and John Rogers found that in all likelihood the frequent migrations of the *statare* were the result of a continuous and often frustrated search for better working, living and especially housing conditions.[64] Was this also true of the 192 families in Borås—large, economically weak and very mobile?

After moving into the houses built for large families these families made, on an average, 0.4 moves per family during an average period of 11.9 years. When migrations are put in relation to time the resulting rate is 30 or not even one move every twentieth year. In other words most of the families did not move at all. This very high rate of persistence may be interpreted as an indication that the large families approved of their new homes, at least—and this might be important—to the extent that they preferred them to any other available housing. One must, of course, remember that these families received rent rebates. Yet, the high persistence rate meant that these families stayed on also after 1948, when rent subsidies generally became available, regardless of where people lived. In this context there was no difference with respect to migrations between the families living in one-family houses and those living in tenement houses.[65] It would appear then that the large families in Borås were satisfied with the new houses and experienced the move to them as an overall improvement.

[63] Five of the 192 families are excluded from these calculations, since death or divorce occurred in conjunction with or soon after the move into the large family houses.
[64] Eriksson–Rogers 1978, pp. 229 ff.
[65] For similar results in a study of subsidised housing, see Pritchard 1976, p. 174.

Table 32. *The large families in Borås: Children moving away from home. Causes of migration*

Cause of migration	Age at migration			All	Per cent
	15–19	20–24	25–29		
Marriage	48	178	56	282	64.1
Per cent	(17.0)	(63.1)	(19.9)	(100)	
Other					
Within Borås	16	33	12	61	13.9
Per cent	(26.2)	(54.1)	(19.7)	(100)	
Outside Borås	36	51	10	97	22.0
Per cent	(37.1)	(52.6)	(10.3)	(100)	
All	100	262	78	440	100
Per cent	(22.7)	(59.6)	(17.7)	(100)	

The negative attitudes of the surrounding society already have been mentioned, together with assumptions of untoward consequences for the children of this kind of separate housing. These assumptions can to some extent be tested by studying migration behaviour with families. Information was excerpted from the population registers on all children who moved away from home during the period of investigation. Furthermore, the nature of the move away from home was considered. Did they move within Borås or to some other place? Did they move away to get married?[66]

As illustrated by Table 32, most moves away from home took place at comparatively high ages and in connection with marriage. The low divorce rates among the parents in these families have already been mentioned. A high sense of family cohesion is further suggested by this study of the children, who tended to stay at home. This of course, might be in accordance with prevailing patterns among working class families.

Concluding Remarks

Theories and research on large families and poverty have often pointed towards a general instability and lack of cohesion within these families. The large families in Borås did not, however, reveal any such tendencies. In fact, the opposite was true. The families appeared to have shown a high degree of appreciation for the special housing for large families. In this essential respect the results of the reform undoubtedly corresponded to the original purpose behind the measure: improved housing for large families.

[66] Since banns of marriage are always recorded in the general population registers of each parish it is possible to determine whether the move took place in connection with marriage or not.

Summary

The main theme of this work has been the study of the implementation and effects of population policies intended to positively affect population development by influencing fertility. The 1930's were years when falling birth rates caused pronatalist demands to be voiced all over Europe. A large, comprehensive population policy program was proposed in Sweden by Alva and Gunnar Myrdal and others and although it was only partially carried out, appeared to have been successful as birth rates began to rise. In order to study the Swedish case in more detail three population policy reforms were chosen for investigation: marriage loans, maternity relief, and improved housing for large families. Particular consideration was given to the correspondence between the intentions of the policymakers and the actual implementation and effects of the reforms.

The marriage loan reform (1937) was adopted from a contemporary German model and was meant to affect fertility by making earlier marriages possible. This would lengthen the fertile period of women within marriage and, it was hoped, increase fertility. In the middle of the 1940's about twenty per cent of the marrying population received marriage loans, enough to make an impact on general fertility possible. The family patterns of 303 recipients of marriage loans in Stockholm in 1942 were investigated. The median age at marriage for women was somewhat lower for this cohort (23) than for the total marrying population (25). About 23 per cent were expecting children when they married—less than the national average of 35 per cent. The divorce rate, however, was high. 27.5 per cent of the marriages were dissolved by divorce, compared to 12 per cent for the total marrying population in 1942.

The family patterns were fairly uniform. In only 27 families were there more than three children. Within the marriages not dissolved by divorce two children were most common. One child was slightly more common than three. Among the divorce cases childlessness was the most frequent pattern. Most children were born during the first ten years of marriage and the time between the parities increased with each successive child. An average of 1.7 children per family were born to the 303 couples. When time is standardised, an average of less than one child per woman was born during a ten year period of marriage. Fertility was thus low among those who received marriage loans and did not, therefore, affect the birth rate significantly.

The marriage loans recipients were found to have an uniform family pattern based on conscious planning. A possible explanation for this might be that they were recruited from the lower middle class/upper working class stratum, i.e. from a group which, according to general social and economic theories on fertility, would be expected to have social and economic aspirations. Such aspirations led them to plan their future and carefully weigh the costs and benefits of children against other potential objectives.

The regulations of the reform required the recipients of loans to be people with a secure income who, if possible, "should have shown an inclination to save". Ironically then the reform appealed to a group which was possibly the least prone to be manipulated with regard to increasing fertility through such an indirect measure as a marriage loan. Politicians and demographic experts were well aware of the appearance of new family strategies and patterns in Sweden in the 1930's. They did not, however, draw the correct conclusions from this knowledge, but rather assumed a simple correlation between length of marriage and number of children. Furthermore, nobody questioned the fact that the loans actually were a way of manipulating people into having more children with least possible cost for the state. The reform was thus not in accordance with the concept of voluntary parenthood which was meant to form the basis of population policy in Sweden in the 1930's.

The maternity relief reform (1937) was to provide temporary economic assistance for childbearing women "in obvious need of help". It was a reform specifically intended for women—something new in this policy area. The reform was directly related to the new abortion law of 1938, which, due to among other things pronatalist considerations was passed in a much stricter from than the original version. The maternity relief reform was enacted to help women in poor circumstances, who might have applied for abortion for social reasons had the more liberal version of the abortion law been adopted. Efforts were made to avoid the social stigma generally attached to poor relief, but a paternalistic attitude of rigid control probably counteracted such efforts.

The need for the reform far surpassed all expectations. In the beginning of the 1940's nearly half of all childbearing women in Sweden received maternity relief. In some parts of northern Sweden, where unemployment rates were very high, more than eighty per cent of all childbearing women received maternity relief. In contrast to other forms of pronatalist support maternity relief was also given to unmarried mothers. A comparison between maternity relief recipients and a control population in a town in central Sweden showed that the fertillity patterns of those who received maternity relief and those who did not, differed significantly. Premarital conception was more frequent among the maternity relief recipients, fertility was higher and family patterns were, in general, more irregular.

136

Maternity relief was expected to affect fertility in a general way. Quantitatively the effect of such a reform is almost impossible to determine and therefore it is unclear whether or not it positively affected fertility. Qualitative effects were also expected and as far as the wellbeing of mother and child are concerned these expectations seem to have been fulfilled.

Improved housing for large families in poor economic circumstances was introduced in 1935 (tenement houses) and in 1938 (one family houses). In 1941 about 9 000 families lived in such housing. 192 families living in tenement houses for large families in a textile town in southwestern Sweden were investigated. The families were by definition large; the average number of children per family was 4.8. Generally they belonged to the lower social strata of the population (mostly unskilled workers, about half of whom were employed in the textile mills). More than eighty per cent of the families had or were expecting children at marriage. The spacing of children was more irregular than, for example, that of the marriage loan recipients. Persistence rates among the families were high. The families generally moved nearly once a year before moving into the special houses for large families. Afterwards, they moved on an average once every twentieth year. Cohesion among these families was also high. Divorce rates were low and children usually did not leave home until they married.

To judge from the behaviour of these families, in particular their high persistence rates, the impact of this reform was on the whole positive. Housing standards were considerably improved for the families concerned. Contemporary opinion, however, worried about the creation of segregated housing and its possible negative consequences. The creation of special housing for large families was therefore stopped in 1948 and replaced by general rent subsidies for low income families regardless of size.

Fertility variations are often studied in relation to social strata. Such studies relate *outer*, "objective" characteristics to behaviour. Criteria for social stratification are coupled to marriage and family behaviour. However, they do not necessarily indicate what class of family pattern individuals and families *identify* with. A working class family, for instance, may very well identify with typical "middle class" patterns. The three population policy measures investigated in this study were selective in two ways. First, they selected certain sections of the population on the basis of outer characteristics. The marriage loan recipients were lower middle class/upper working class. The large families and those who received maternity relief were of poorer circumstances. There was also a selectivity in relation to subjective identification. For instance, those who received marriage loans and belonged to the unskilled working class also displayed characteristics suggesting a pattern of rational planning, long time horizons and a "middle class" mentality. Those selected for reasons of com-

137

parative poverty, on the other hand, displayed characteristics suggesting a sense of helplessness and a non-planning behaviour.

Modern Swedish social policy to a considerable extent originates in the population policies designed in the 1930's. Studying the people affected by such policies has made it necessary to establish a theoretical distinction between social policies and population policies. Population policies generally treat human beings as *means*, whereas in a social policy context they are regarded as *ends*. The relationship between population policy motives and social policy motives and the influence of population policy on social policy therefore must be ascertained and investigated. In Sweden in the 1930's the inherent conflict between social policy and population policy goals is discernible, particularly in the writings of Alva and Gunnar Myrdal. Swedish pronatalist demands led to a social policy concentrated on the family and to the creation of reforms that, in practice, did not conform to the officially proclaimed ideal of voluntary parenthood. Although for years the Swedish population policies of the 1930's have been considered successful, the results of this study indicate that the pronatalist goals were, at best, only partially realised.

Bibliography

I. Unpublished Sources

Riksarkivet (National Archives, Stockholm).
 Socialdepartementet (Ministry of Social Affairs).
  Konseljakter
  Kommitté nr 542
   1935 års befolkningskommission (The 1935 Committee on Population).
  Kommitté nr 864: 9
   Besparingsberedningens handlingar (Proceedings of the Committee on Retrench-
   ment).
    *PM angående lån och bidrag av statsmedel för beredande av hyresbostäder åt mindre
    bemedlade, barnrika familjer* (PM on loans and grants for housing for less well-
    to-do couples with large families).
    Skrivelse och PM angående statens bosättningslån (Communication and PM on
    marriage loans).
  Kommitté nr 1425
   1933 års bostadssociala utredning (The 1933 Commission on Social Housing).
  Kommitté nr 1671
   1941 års befolkningsutredning (The 1941 Population Commission).
Sveriges Riksbank. Bosättningslåneavdelningen, Stockholm (National Bank of Sweden. Depart-
 ment for marriage loans, Stockholm).
 Diarium över bosättningslån (Diary, marriage loans).
 Register över bosättningslån 1938–1944 (Register of marriage loans 1938–1944).
 Statistik över bosättningslån 1/1 1938–30/6 1948 (Statistics on marriage loans).
Statistiska centralbyråns arkiv (Archives of the Central Bureau of Statistics, Stockholm).
 Socialstyrelsens fjärde byrå (The Social Welfare Board, Fourth Division).
 Mödrahjälpsstatistik (Maternity relief statistics).
 Socialstyrelsens femte byrå (The Social Welfare Board, Fifth Division).
 Bostäderna för barnrika familjer (Housing for large families).
 Folkräkningen 1940 (The Census of 1940).
 Utdrag ur husförhörslängder (Nominative extracts from catechetical examination
 records).
Befolkningsregistret, Stockholm (The Population Register in Stockholm).
Uppsala läns landstings arkiv (Uppsala County Council).
 Mödrahjälpsnämndens protokoll (The Maternity Assistance Board: Minutes).
Borås stadsarkiv (Borås Municipal Archives).
 AB Egna Hem: Minutes and other records.
Mörbylånga kommunarkiv (Mörbylånga Municipal Archives).
 Barnavårdsnämndens protokoll (The Child Welfare Committee: Minutes).
 Fattigvårdsstyrelsens protokoll (The Public Assistance Board: Minutes).
Revsunds kommunarkiv (Revsund Municipal Archives).
 Barnavårdsnämndens protokoll (The Child Welfare Committee: Minutes).
 Fattigvårdsstyrelsens protokoll (The Public Assistance Board: Minutes).

Uppsala stadsarkiv (Uppsala Municipal Archives).
Fattigvårdsstyrelsens protokoll (The Public Assistance Board: Minutes).
Åmål kommunarkiv (Åmål Municipal Archives).
Barnavårdsnämndens protokoll (The Child Welfare Committee: Minutes).
Fattigvårdsstyrelsens protokoll (The Public Assistance Board: Minutes).

Parish Archives

Adelsö, Alingsås, Almby, Axberg, Bollsta-Näs, Borgstena, Borås Caroli, Borås Gustaf Adolf, Botkyrka, Bredared, Bro (Stockholms *län*), Bro (Uppsala *län*). Bromma, Brämhult, Brännkyrka, Danderyd, Ed (Stockholms *län*), Edefors, Enskede, Eskilstuna, Essinge, Falkenberg, Fredriksberg, Fresta, Fristad, Fjärdhundra, Forsa (Södermanlands *län*). Färentuna, Gamla Uppsala, Gingri, Grödinge, Gustafsberg, Gävle, Göteborgs domkyrkoförsamling, Göteborg Gamlestad, Göteborg Haga, Göteborg Vasa, Göteborg Örgryte, Halmstad, Hammarby, Herrljunga, Hille (Gävleborgs *län*), Horred, Huddinge, Hudiksvall, Husby-Rekarne, Hyssna, Hägersten, Härnösand, Härryda, Häverö, Järfälla, Kalmar, Karl Gustaf, Kinnared, Kinnarum, Kristinehamn, Kärnbo, Kävsjö, Lena, Lidingö, Linköpings domkyrkoförsamling, Ljungarp, Ljungby (Kalmar *län*), Ljusdal, Lovö, Ludgo, Ludvika, Lundby, Malmberget, Malmö Slottsstaden, Markaryd, Mariefred, Mariestad, Munsö, Märsta, Mölndal, Nacka, Norrköping Hedvig, Norrköping Olai, Norrsunda, Nyköping, Nynäshamn, Näslunda, Nässjö, Od, Oskarshamn, Piteå, Rasbo (Uppsala *län*), Riseberga, Saltsjöbaden, Saltsjö-Boo, Sandhult, Seglora, Sigtuna, Simtuna, Skerid, Skå, Skånes Fagerhult, Skönsmon (Västernorrlands *län*), Skövde, Spånga, Sollentuna, Solna, Sorunda, Stockholm Sofia, Strängnäs, Sundbyberg, Sundsvall, Surahammar, Svenljunga, Sånga, Säby, Södertälje, Södra Ving, Tierp, Toarp, Toresund, Torshälla landsförsamling, Trelleborg, Trollhättan, Tullinge, Tumba, Tyresö, Tysslinge, Täby, Uddevalla, Ullasjö, Ulricehamn, Udenäs, Upplands Väsby, Uppsala domkyrkoförsamling, Uppsala Helga Trefaldighet, Valbo, Valdermarsvik, Vallby (Uppsala *län*), Varnum, Vendelsö, Väddö, Värmdö, Vännäs, Värnamo, Västerås domkyrkoförsamling, Ytterselö, Åby (Kalmar *län*), Åkersberga, Åsele, Åsle, Älvsered, Älvsjö, Örebro Nikolai, Örebro Olaus Petri, Össeby-Garn, Österhaninge, Österåker, Östra Ryd, Överluleå.

HSB:s arkiv, Borås (Archive of the Tenants' Savings and Building Society, Borås).

Protokoll, årsredogörelser, övriga handlingar (Minutes, annual reports and other records).

II. Books and Articles, Published and Unpublished

AB Egna Hem i Borås, 1914–1965
Borås 1965

Alegård, G., *Svensk befolkningspolitik förr och nu*. Skrifter utgivna av Nationalekonomiska föreningen i Skåne, III. (Swedish population policy past and present.) Malmö 1941. [Alegård 1941.]

Andorka, R., *Determinants of Fertility in Advanced Countries*. London 1978. [Andorka 1978.]

Armengaud, A., "Mouvement ouvrier et néo-malthusianisme au début de XXe siècle." *Annales de Démographie Historique* 1966. [Armengaud 1966.]

Askham, Janet, *Fertility and Deprivation. A Study of Differential Fertility amongst Working-class Families in Aberdeen*. Cambridge 1975. [Askham 1975.]

Beaujeu-Garnier, Jacqueline, *La population française.* Paris 1969. [Beaujeu-Garnier 1969.]

"Bankoutskottets memorial 1938, 1939." (Memorandum of the Standing Committee on Banking and Currency.) In *Riksdagstrycket* (Sweden's parliamentary papers). [*Bankoutskottets memorial.*]

Berelson, B. (ed.), *Population Policy in Developed Countries.* New York 1974. [Berelson 1974.]

Bergman, Elihu, "Values and Choices: Some Anomalies in American Population Policy Making" in Clinton, Richard L. (ed.), *Population and Politics. New Directions in Political Science Research.* Toronto–London 1973. [Bergman 1973.]

Bernhardt, Eva, *Trends and Variations in Swedish Fertility. A Cohort Study.* Stockholm 1971. [Bernhardt 1971.]

Berättelse över statens byggnadslånebyrås verksamhet under budgetåret 1947/48. (Annual report of the National Housing Loan Office, 1947/48).

Bickel, W., *Bevölkerungsgeschichte und Bevölkerungspolitik der Schweiz seit der Ausgang des Mittelalters.* Zürich 1947. [Bickel 1947.]

The Biography of a People. Past and Future Population Changes in Sweden. Conditions and Consequences. (Royal Ministry of Foreign Affairs.) Stockholm 1974. [The Biography of a People.]

Blake, Judith, "Coercive Pronatalism and American Population Policy" in Kammeyer, Kenneth C. W., *Population Studies. Selected Essays and Research.* Chicago 1975. [Blake 1975.]

— "Population Policies." *International Encyclopedia of the Social Sciences.* 1968. [Blake 1968.]

— "Reproductive Motivation and Population Policy." *Bio-science*, 21: 5, 1971. [Blake 1971.]

— "Is Zero Preferred? American Attitudes Towards Childlessness in the 1970s". *Journal of Marriage and the Family*, 1979. [Blake 1979.]

Blayo, Chantal, "Facteurs economiques et sociaux à l'origine du declin de la fecondité et de l'arret de la croissance dans les pays developpés." *9e Congrès Mondial de Sociologie*, Uppsala, Suède, 1978. [Blayo 1978.]

Boberg, K., Lorentzon, M., Lundgren, R., Löwendahl, B., Modh, B., Nilsson, K. & Wikner, C.-E., *Bostad och kapital. En studie av svensk bostadspolitik,* (Housing and capital. A study of Swedish housing policy.) Lund 1974. [Boberg et alii 1974.]

Borås kommunalblad. (Borås Municipal Newsletter.)

Borås Wäfveri Aktiebolag, 1870–1945. (The Borås Weaving Co.) Stockholm 1945.

Bourgeois-Pichat, Jean, "France" in Berelson, B. (ed.), *Population Policy in Developed Countries.* New York 1974. [Bourgeois-Pichat 1974.]

Burgdörfer, Friedrich, *Geburtenschwund. Die Kulturkrankheit Europas und ihre Überwindung in Deutschland.* Heidelberg–Berlin–Magdeburg 1942. [Burgdörfer 1942.]

del Campo, Salustiano, "Spain" in Berelson, B. (ed.), *Population Policy in Developed Countries.* New York 1974. [del Campo 1974.]

Carlsson, Sten, *Fröknar, mamseller, jungfrur och pigor. Ogifta kvinnor i det svenska ståndssamhället.* (Unmarried women in the Swedish society of estates.) Studia Historica Upsaliensia 90. Acta Universitatis Upsaliensis. Uppsala 1977. [S. Carlsson 1977.]

Carlsson, Gösta, "The Decline in Fertility: Innovation or Adjustment Process." *Population Studies*, 20, 1966. [G. Carlsson 1966.]

Carlsson, Lizzie, "Äkenskapets ingående enligt äldre rätt." (Contracting marriage according to early law.) *Fataburen* 1969. [L. Carlsson 1969.]

141

Ceccaldi, Dominique, *Histoire des prestations familiales en France*. Paris 1957. [Ceccaldi 1957.]

Cederström-Friman, H., Henschen, H., Högberg, L., Silvén-Garnert, E., Söderlind, I. & Bjurman, E. L., *Barn i stan från sekelskifte till sjuttiotal*. (City children from the turn of the century to the seventies.) Kristianstad 1979. [Cederström *et alii* 1979.]

Cervin, Ulf, *Barnrikehusen. Några preliminära resultat samt förslag till forsknings-uppgifter*. (Housing for large families. Some preliminary results and proposals for research.) Unpublished paper. Dept. of History, University of Lund, 1974. [Cervin 1974.]

— "Makarna Myrdal och befolkningsfrågan." (The Myrdals and the population question.) Unpublished paper. Dept. of History, University of Lund, 1971. [Cervin 1971.]

Cherlin, Andrew, "The Effect of Children on Marital Dissolution." *Demography*, 14: 3, 1977. [Cherlin 1977.]

Checkland, S. G. & E. O. A., "Introduction" in Checkland, S. G. & E. O. A. (eds.), *The Poor Law Report of 1834*. Harmondsworth 1974. [Checkland 1974.]

Clinton, Richard L., "Population, Politics, and Political Science" in Clinton, Richard L. (ed.), *Population and Politics. New Directions in Political Science Research*. Toronto–London 1973. [Clinton 1973.]

Dahlström, Edmund, *Trivsel i Söderort. Sociologisk undersökning i Hägerstensåsen och Hökmossen 1949–50*. (Sociological investigation in H. and H. 1949–1950.) Stockholm 1951. [Dahlström 1951.]

Davin, Anna, "Imperialism and Motherhood." *History Workshop—A Journal of Socialist Historians* 5: 1978. [Davin 1978.]

Dore, Grazia, *La democrazia Italiana e l'emigrazione in America*. Brescia 1964. [Dore 1964.]

Dovring, F., *Agrarhistorien*. (Agrarian history.) Stockholm 1953. [Dovring 1953.]

Dungel, Bengt Rune (ed.), *150 år med Borås Tidning. Tidnings- och händelsekrönika 1826–1976*. (150 years with the "Borås Tidning" Newspaper.) Borås 1976. [Dungel 1976.]

Dyring, Nils (ed.), *Samverkan gav goda bostäder. Minnesskrift i anledning av "Hyresgästernas Sparkasse- och Byggnadsförening"*. (Cooperation gave good housing. Memorial publication for 'The Tenants' Savings & Building Society'.) Borås 1944. [Dyring 1944.]

Easterlin, R., "The Economics and Sociology of Fertility" in Tilly, C. (ed.), *Historical Studies of Changing Fertility*. Princeton 1976. [Easterlin 1976.]

Edin, Karl A.–Hutchinson, Edw. P., *Studies of Differential Fertility in Sweden*. London 1935. [Edin–Hutchinson 1935.]

Elmér, Åke, *Från Fattigsverige till välfärdsstaten*. (From impoverished Sweden to the welfare state.) Lund 1975. [Elmér 1975.]

Elster, Jon, "Några metodproblem i ekonomisk historia" (Some methodological problems in economic history) in Norén, K., *Människans samhälleliga vara; marxistisk forskningsteori i humanistisk forskning*. Staffanstorp 1973. [Elster 1973.]

Emigrationsutredningen. Bilaga I. Utvandringslagstiftningen. Öfversikt af dess utveckling och nuvarande beskaffenhet i Europas olika stater. (Committee on Emigration. Survey of its development and present situation in different European countries.) Stockholm 1908.

— *Bilaga V. Bygdestatistik*. (Regional statistics.) Stockholm 1910.

Eriksson, Ingrid–Rogers, John, *Rural Labor and Population Change. Social and Demographic Developments in East-central Sweden during the Nineteenth Century*. Studia Historica Upsaliensia 100. Uppsala 1978. [Eriksson–Rogers 1978.]

142

Fauchille, F., *Traité de droit international publique.* Paris 1922. [Fauchille 1922.]

Flinn, M. W., "The English Population Scare of the 1930's" in Kovacsics, J. (ed.), *Historisch-Demographische Mitteilungen.* Budapest 1976. [Flinn 1976.]

Folkräkningen den 31 december 1930. IX. Äktenskap och barnantal. (Recensement de la population en 1930 par le Bureau Central de Statistique. IX. Mariage et Nombre d'Enfants.) Stockholm 1939.

Freedman, Ronald, "The Sociology of Human Fertility" in Ford, Thomas R. and De Jong, Gordon F. (ed.), *Social Demography.* Englewood Cliffs 1970. [Freedman 1970.]

Friberg, Arthur, *Borås textilare 1949–1969.* (Textile weavers in Borås, 1949–1969.) Borås 1969. [Friberg 1969.]

Gille, H., "Families Welfare Measures in Denmark." *Population Studies,* Vol. III, 1953. [Gille 1953.]

Glass, D. V., *Population Policies and Movements in Europe.* London 1940. New Ed. London 1967. [Glass 1940.]

Godwin, B. Kenneth, "Methodology and Policy" in Clinton, Richard L. (ed.), *Population and Politics. New Directions in Political Science Research.* Toronto–London 1973. [Godwin 1973.]

Gonäs, Lena, "Kris i befolkningsfrågan?" (Crisis in the population question?) in *Förr och nu,* 2 1978. (Then and Now.) [Gonäs 1978.]

Gregory, J. W., *Human Migration and the Future. A Study of the Causes, Effects and Control of Emigration.* London 1928. [Gregory 1928.]

Guillebaud, C. W., *The Social Policy of Nazi Germany.* Cambridge 1941. [Guillebaud 1941.]

Gustafsson, Bo under medverkan av Erkki Pihkala och Kåre D. Tönnesson, "Perspektiv på den offentliga sektorn under 1930-talet" (Views on the Public Sector during the 1930's) in *Kriser och krispolitik i Norden under mellankrigstiden. Nordiska historikermötet i Uppsala 1974. Mötesrapport.* (Crises and crisis policy in the Nordic countries between the wars. Proceedings of the Meeting of Nordic Historians, Uppsala 1974.) Uppsala 1974. [Gustafsson 1974.]

Gårdlund, Torsten, *Industrialismens samhälle. De svenska arbetarklassens historia.* (The industrial society. History of the Swedish working class). Stockholm 1942. [Gårdlund 1942.]

— *Knut Wicksell. Rebell i det nya riket.* (Knut Wicksell. Rebel in the new kingdom.) Stockholm 1956. [Gårdlund 1956.]

Hafström, Gerhard, *Den svenska familjerättens historia.* (History of Swedish family rights.) Lund 1970. [Hafström 1970.]

Hammar, Tomas, *Sverige åt svenskarna. Invandringspolitik, utlänningskontroll och asylrätt 1900–1932.* (Sweden for the Swedes. Immigration policy, alien control and right to asylum, 1900–1932.) Stockholm 1964. [Hammar 1964.]

Hamrin, Agne, *Italienarnas Italien.* (Italy of the Italians.) Stockholm 1965. [Hamrin 1965.]

Hatje, Ann-Katrin, "Befolkningsdebattens betydelse för statsmakternas befolkningspolitiska strävanden under slutet av 1800-talet fram till 1900-talet". (Importance of the population debate for the aims of official population policy from the late 1800's until the 1900's). In *Forskare om befolkningsfrågor. Blandvetenskaplig bilaga till Ett Folks Biografi.* (In Researchers on population questions. Multidisciplinary contribution to the Biography of a People.) Stockholm 1975. [Hatje 1975.]

— *Befolkningsfrågan och välfärden. Debatten om familjepolitik och nativitetsökning under 1930- och 1940-talen.* (The population question and welfare. Debate on family policy and increased birth rate during the 1930's and 1940's.) Stockholm 1974. [Hatje 1974.]

Hawthorn, Geoffrey, *The Sociology of Fertility*. London 1970. [Hawthorn 1970.]

— *Population Policy: A Modern Delusion*. Fabian tract 418. London 1973. [Hawthorn 1973.]

Heckscher, E. F., *Mercantilism*, 2 Vols. London 1935. [Heckscher 1935.]

— *Svenskt arbete och liv från medeltiden till nutiden*. (Swedish work and life from the Middle Ages until the present.) Stockholm 1941. [Heckscher 1941.]

— *Sveriges ekonomiska historia från Gustav Vasa. Andra delen. Det moderna Sveriges grundläggning*. (Swedish economic history since Gustavus Vasa. Part II. The foundation of modern Sweden.) Stockholm 1949. [Heckscher 1949.]

Historisk statistik för Sverige. Del 1. Befolkningen 1720–1967. (Historical Statistics of Sweden. Part 1. Population 1720–1967.) Andra upplagan. Stockholm 1969.

"History of Population Theories". By the Population Division, United Nations, in Spengler, J. J. and Duncan, O. D. (eds.) *Population Theory and Policy*. Glencoe 1956. [History of Population Theories.]

Hofsten, Erland, "Kohortvisa och periodvisa skeenden". (Longitudinal and periodic processes.) *Statistisk tidskrift* 1975: 2. [Hofsten 1975.]

Hofsten, E. –Lundström, H., *Swedish Population History. Main Trends from 1750–1970*. Stockholm 1976. [Hofsten–Lundström 1976.]

Holm, Per, "Bostadsmarknad, bostadsteori och bostadspolitik—ett historiskt perspektiv". (The housing market, housing theory and housing policy—an historical perspicitive.) in *Samhället som det blev. Uppsatser om boende, bostadspolitik och bostadsproduktion*. (Essays on housing, housing policies and housing production.) Stockholm 1976. [Holm 1976.]

Holmberg, Per, "Svensk socialpolitik — nuläge och tendenser." (Swedish social policy —present situation and trends.) Unpublished paper, Stockholm 1974. [Holmberg 1974.]

Hutchinson, E. P., *The Population Debate. The Development of Conflicting Theories up to 1900*. Boston 1967. [Hutchinson 1967.]

Hvidt, K., *Flugten til Amerika eller Drivekræfter i masseudvandringen fra Danmark 1868–1914*. (The flight to America or push factors in mass emigration from Denmark.) Odense 1971. [Hvidt 1971.]

Hyrenius, H., "The Relation Between Birth Rates and Economic Activity in Sweden 1920–1944." *Bulletin of the Oxford University. Institute of Statistics*. Vol. 8. 1946. [Hyrenius 1946.]

Hörsell, A. – Nelson, Marie, C., "Smeder och änkor." (Smiths and their widows.) *Sörmlandsbygden* 1980. [Hörsell–Nelson 1980.]

Isacson, Maths, Ekonomisk tillväxt och social differentiering 1680–1860. (Economic development and social differentiation.) Uppsala 1979. [Isacson 1979.]

Iverus, I., *Versuch einer Darstellung des Zusammenhanges zwischen Bevölkerungsentwicklung, Familienpolitik und öffentlicher Meinung in Schweden*. Helsingfors 1953. [Iverus 1953.]

Jobst, W., *Bevölkerungspolitische Auswirkungen der Ehestandsdarlehen*. Archiv für Bevölkerungswissenschaft und Bevölkerungspolitik, 1940. [Jobst 1940.]

Johansson, Alf, "Bostadspolitiken". (Housing policy.) In *Hundra år under kommunalförfattningarna 1862–1962. En minnesskrift utgiven av Svenska Landskommunernas Förbund, Svenska Landstingsförbundet, Svenska stadsförbundet*. (In A century under municipal constitution, 1862–1962.) Stockholm 1962. [Johansson 1962.]

Johnston, H. J. M., *British Emigration Policy. 1815–1830. "Shovelling out Paupers"*. Oxford 1972. [Johnston 1972.]

144

Jonsson, Lena, "Sweden" in Berelson, B. (ed.), *Population Policy in Developed Countries*. New York 1974. [Jonsson 1974.]

Kammeyer, Kenneth C. W., "Population Politics and Policies. Introduction: A. Population Policy: National and Worldwide" in Kammeyer, Kenneth C. W. (ed.), *Population Studies. Selected Essays and Research*. Chicago 1975. [Kammeyer 1975.]

Knodel, John E., *The Decline of Fertility in Germany, 1871–1939*. Princeton 1974. [Knodel 1974.]

— "Age Patterns of Fertility and the Fertility Transition: Evidence from Europe and Asia." *Population Studies*, 31, 1977. [Knodel 1977.]

Koehl, Robert L., *RKFDV: German Resettlement and Population Policy, 1939–1945. A History of the Reich Commission for the Strengthening of Germandom*. Cambridge, Mass., 1957. [Koehl 1957.]

Konferens i Stockholm rörande mödrahjälpsnämndernas verksamhet. (Conference in Stockholm on the work of the Maternity Assistance Boards.) Stockholm 1939. [*Konferens i Stockholm etc.*]

Kuusi, Pekka, *Social Policy for the Sixties. A Plan for Finland*. Kuopio 1964. [Kuusi 1964.]

Kälvemark, Ann-Sofie, *Reaktionen mot utvandringen. Emigrationsfrågan i svensk debatt och politik 1901–1904*. (The Swedish reaction against emigration. The issue of emigration in Swedish debate and politics 1901–04.) Studia Historica Upsaliensia 41. Uppsala 1972. [Kälvemark 1972.]

— "Swedish Emigration Policy in an International Perspective" in Runblom, H.–Norman, H. (eds.), *From Sweden to America. A History of the Migration*. Uppsala 1976. [Kälvemark 1976.]

— "The Country That Kept Track of Its Population. Methodological Aspects of Swedish Population Records." *Scandinavian Journal of History*, 1977. [Kälvemark 1977:1.]

— "Den uteblivna motprestationen. Bosättningslånen i 1930-talets svenska befolkningspolitik." (Marriage loans in Swedish population policy of the 1930's.) In Tedebrand, L.-G. *(ed)*, *Historieforskning på nya vägar. Studier tillägnade Sten Carlson 14.12.1977*. (New approaches in historical research. Studies dedicated to Sten Carlsson 14.12.1977.) Lund 1977. [Kälvemark 1977:2.]

— "Att vänta barn när man gifter sig. Föräktenskapliga förbindelser och giftermålsmönster i 1800-talets Sverige." (Premarital pregnancy. Premarital relationships and marriage patterns in 19th century Sweden.) *Historisk tidskrift* 1977. [Kälvemark 1977:3.]

— "Äktenskap och familj i Sverige i historiskt perspektiv." (Marriage and family in Sweden in an historical perspective.) *Historielärarnas Förenings Årsskrift* 1977/78. [Kälvemark 1978.]

— "Illegitimacy and Marriage in Three Swedish Parishes in the Nineteenth Century." In Laslett, P., Oosterveen, K., and Smith, R. M., *Bastardy and its Comparative History*. London 1980. [Kälvemark 1980.]

Langholm, Sivert, "On the Scope of Micro-History." *Scandinavian Journal of History*, 1976, Vol. 1. No. 1–2. [Langholm 1976.]

Lannerberth, O., "Angående samarbete mellan barnavårdsnämnderna och mödrahjälpsnämnden." (On the cooperation between Child Welfare Committees and the Maternity Assistance Boards.) *Svensk fattigvårds- och barnavårds tidning* 1941:4. [Lannerberth 1941:1.]

— "Har en barnavårdsnämnd laglig rätt att åt en särskild delegation överlåta sin skyldighet att avgiva yttranden i mödrahjälpsärenden?" (Does the Child Welfare

Committee have the legal right to transfer its obligations to submit statements on matters concerning maternity relief?) *Svensk fattigvårds- och barnavårds tidning* 1941: 7. [Lannerberth 1941: 2.]

Laslett, Peter, "Familie und Industrialisierung: eine "starke Theorie" in Conze, Werner (Hrsg.), *Sozialgeschichte der Familie in der Neuzeit Europas*. Stuttgart 1976. [Laslett 1976.]

Lehmann, Sylvia, *Grundzüge der schweizerischen Auswanderungspolitik*. Bern 1949. [Lehmann 1949.]

Lestaeghe, R., "The Feasability of Controlling Population Growth Through Nuptiality and Nuptiality Policies" in *International Population Conference. Liège 1973*. Vol. 3. Liège 1973. [Lestaeghe 1973.]

Lewin, Bo, *Om ogift samboende i Sverige med tonvikt på samtida förhållanden*. (On cohabitation outside marriage in Sweden, with emphasis on the contemporary situation.) Uppsala 1979. [Lewin 1979.]

Liljeström, Rita, *A Study of Abortion in Sweden*. Stockholm 1974. [Liljeström 1974.]

Lincoln, Richard, "Population and the American Future: The Commission's Final Report" in Kammeyer, Kenneth W. C. (ed.), *Population Studies: Selected Essays and Research*. Chicago 1975. [Lincoln 1975.]

Lipsitz, Lewis, "Political Philosophy and Population Policy. Insights and Blindspots of a Tradition" in Clinton, Richard L. (ed.), *Political Science in Population Studies*. Toronto–London 1977. [Lipsitz 1977.]

Livi-Bacci, Massimo, "Italy" in Berelson, B. (ed.), *Population Policy in Developed Countries*. New York 1974. [Livi-Bacci 1974: 1.]

— "Population Policy in Western Europe." *Population Studies*, Vol. 28, 1974. [Livi-Bacci 1974: 2.]

Lohlé-Tart, Louis, "Belgium" in Berelson, B. (ed.), *Population Policy in Developed Countries*. New York 1974. [Lohlé-Tart 1974.]

Lundevall, Owe, "HSB:s utveckling under 40 år." (Development of the National Association of Tenants' Savings and Building Society during 40 years.) In *Samhället som det blev. Uppsatser om boende, bostadspolitik och bostadsproduktion*. (Essays on housing, housing policies and housing production.) Stockholm 1976. [Lundevall 1976.]

Lyons, Thomas E., "Population Policy: The Ethical Dimension" in Clinton, Richard L. (ed.), *Population and Politics. New Directions in Political Science Research*. Toronto–London 1973. [Lyons 1973.]

Löfgren, Orvar, "Från nattfrieri till tonårskult." (From bundling to teen-age culture.) *Fataburen* 1969. [Löfgren 1969.]

— Fångstmän i industrisamhället. En halländsk kustbygds omvandling 1800–1970. (Fishermen in the industrial society. The transformation of a coastal area of Halland, West Sweden, 1800–1970.) Lund 1977. [Löfgren 1977.]

Macura, M., "Population Policies in Socialist Countries of Europe." *Population Studies*, 1974. [Macura 1974.]

Martinius, S., *Peasant Destinies. The History of 552 Swedes Born 1810–12*. Stockholm 1977. [Martinius 1977.]

Meadows, Paul, "Towards a Socialized Population Policy" in Spengler, J. J. and Duncan, O. D. (eds.), *Population Policy and Theory*. Glencoe 1956. [Meadows 1956.]

Meddelanden från Kungl. Socialstyrelsens byrå för fattigvårds- och barnavårdsärenden m. m. (Bulletin from the National Social Welfare Board's Division for poor relief and child welfare.)

Meidner, Rudolf, "Befolkningspolitikens effekt på den demografiska utvecklingen i

Tyskland 1933–39." *Bil. 2. 1941 års befolkningsutredning. SOU* 1944:26. (Effect of population policy on demographic development in Germany, 1933–39.) [Meidner 1944.]

Montgomery, Arthur, *The Rise of Modern Industry in Sweden.* Stockholm Economic Studies 8. London 1939. [Montgomery 1939.]

Muresan, Petre–Copil, Joan M., "Romania" in Berelson, B. (ed.), *Population Policy in Developed Countries.* New York 1974. [Muresan–Copil 1974.]

Mundebo, Ingemar, *Ny kris i befolkningsfrågan?* (New crisis in the population question?) Uddevalla 1962. [Mundebo 1962.]

Myrdal, Alva, "A programme for family security in Sweden." *International Labour Review*, 1939. [A. Myrdal 1939.]

— *Nation and Family. The Swedish Experiment in Democratic Family and Population Policy.* London 1941. [A. Myrdal 1941.]

— *Folk och familj.* (People and family.) Stockholm 1944. [A. Myrdal 1944.]

Myrdal, Alva–Myrdal, Gunnar, *Kris i befolkningsfrågan.* (Crisis in the population question.) Stockholm 1934. [A. and G. Myrdal 1934.]

Myrdal, Gunnar, "Population Problems and Policies." *Annals Am. Acad. Pol. and Social Science*, 1938. [G. Myrdal 1938.]

— *Population—A Problem for Democracy.* Gloucester (Mass.) 1940, repr. 1962. [G. Myrdal 1940.]

Myrdal, Gunnar–Åhrén, Uno, *Bostadsfrågan som socialt planläggningsproblem.* The problem of housing as a problem of social planning.) Stockholm 1933. [Myrdal–Åhrén 1933.]

Nasenius, Jan–Ritter, Kristin, *Delad välfärd. Svensk socialpolitik förr och nu.* (Shared welfare. Swedish social policy then and now.) Stockholm 1974. [Nasenius–Ritter 1974.]

Nash, A. E. Keir, "Political Values, Policy Making, and Problem Solving: Political Science Issues in Population Studies" in Clinton, Richard L. (ed.), *Population and Politics. New Directions in Political Science Research.* Toronto–London 1973. [Nash 1973.]

Nevéus, Torgny, *Sörmlandstinget 1938–1965.* (The Sörmland Assizes, 1938–1965.) Nyköping 1972. [Nevéus 1972.]

Nilsson, Göran B., *100 års landstingspolitik. Västmanlands läns landsting 1863–1963.* (A century of county council politics. Västmanland *län* county council 1863–1963.) Uppsala 1966. [Nilsson 1966.]

Odén, Birgitta, "Individuella tidshorisonter." (Individual time horizons.) In *Forskare om befolkningsfrågor. Blandvetenskaplig bilaga till Ett Folks Biografi.* (In Researchers on population questions. Multidisciplinary contribution to the Biography of a People.) Stockholm 1975. [Odén 1975.]

Overbeek, J., *History of Population Theories.* Rotterdam 1974. [Overbeek 1974.]

Pavlik, Zdenek–Wynnyczuk, Vladimir, "Czechoslovakia" in Berelson, B. (ed.), *Population Policy in Developed Countries.* New York 1974. [Pavlik–Wynnyczuk 1974.]

Persson, H., *Svenska beklädnadsarbetareförbundets avdelning 67 i Borås, 1917–1942.* (Swedish Clothing Workers' Union, sect. 67 in Borås, 1917–1942.) Borås 1942. [Persson 1942.]

Petersen, William, *Population.* New York 1969. [Petersen 1969.]

Piepponen, Paavo, "Finland" in Berelson, B. (ed.), *Population Policy in Developed Countries.* New York 1974. [Piepponen 1974.]

Pinker, Robert, *Social Theory & Social Policy.* London 1971. [Pinker 1971.]

Population Movements and Industrialization, Swedish Counties 1895–1930. Stockholm Economic Studies 10: 1. Stockholm 1941. [Population Movements.]

Pressat, Roland, *Population.* Harmondsworth 1970. [Pressat 1970.]

Pritchard, R. M., *Housing and the Spatial Structure of the City. Residential Mobility and the Housing Market in an English City Since the Industrial Revolution.* Cambridge 1976. [Pritchard 1976.]

Quensel, C.-E., "Barnantalet i de svenska äktenskapen 1936." (Numbers of children in Swedish marriages 1936.) *Statsvetenskaplig tidskrift* 1936: 3. [Quensel 1936.]

— "Giftermålsintensiteten i Sverige under de sista årtiondena och dess framtida storlek." (Marriage rates in Sweden during recent decades and its future magnitude.) *Statsvetenskaplig tidskrift* 1939: 2. [Quensel 1939.]

Rahlfs, H., *Fruchtbarkeit der Ehen mit und ohne Ehestandsdarlehen.* Archiv für Bevölkerungswissenschaft und Bevölkerungspolitik, 1940. [Rahlfs 1940.]

Rainwater, Lee, *And the Poor Get Children. Sex, Contraception and Family Planning in the Working Class.* Chicago 1960. [Rainwater 1960.]

Rein, Martin, *Social Policy: Issues of Choice and Change.* New York 1970. [Rein 1970.]

Reinders, Frank, *Möglichkeiten und Grenzen der Messung der Bevölkerungsreproduktion mittels Reproduktionsziffern und Kohortenanalyse.* Tübingen 1970. [Reinders 1970.]

— "Zur Geburtenentwicklung in Deutschland zwischen 1933 und 1940." *Allgemeines Statistisches Archiv. Organ der deutschen statistischen Gesellschaft,* 3: 1974. [Reinders 1974.]

Reinhard, M., Armengaud, A. & Dupaquier, J., *Histoire générale de la population mondiale.* Paris 1968. [Reinhard *et alii* 1968.]

Reynolds, Jack, "Measuring the Demographic Effectiveness of Antinatalist Policies" in *International Population Conference,* vol. 3, Liège 1973. [Reynolds 1973.]

"Riksdagens revisorers berättelse. Del I, 1939 års revisionsberättelse angående statsverket. Del II, Förklaringar." (Report of the parliamentary auditors. Part I. The 1939 report on the public administration. Part II. Explanations.) In *Bihang till lagtima riksdagens protokoll 1940: 2: 1.* (Appendix to the statutory parliamentary session, 1940: 2: 1.)

Riksdagstrycket. (Sweden's Parliamentary Papers.)

Runeby, Nils, "Amerika i Sverige. Herman Lagercrantz, emitration och den nationella väckelsen." (America in Sweden. H. L., emigration and the antional revival movement.) *Arkivvetenskapliga studier,* 3. Lund 1962. [Runeby 1962.]

Ryder, Norman B., "The Cohort as a Concept in the Study of Social Change" in Ford, Thomas R. and De Jong, Gordon F., *Social Demography.* Englewood Cliffs 1970. [Ryder 1970.]

Samuelsson, Kurt, *From Great Power to Welfare State. 300 years of Swedish Social Development.* London 1968. [Samuelsson 1968.]

Sanger, Margaret (ed.), *Proceedings of the World Population Conference.* London 1927. [Sanger 1927.]

Schofield, Roger, "The Relationship Between Demographic Structure and Environment in Pre-industrial Western Europe" in Conze, Werner (Hrsg.), *Sozialgeschichte der Familie in der Neuzeit Europas.* Stuttgart 1976. [Schofield 1976.]

Schubnell, Herman, "West Germany" in Berelson, B. (ed.), *Population Policy in Developed Countries.* New York 1974. [Schubnell 1974.]

Schultz, Th. W., "Fertility and Economic Values" in Schultz, Th. W., *Economics and the Family. Marriage, Children and Human Capital.* Chicago 1974. [Schultz 1974.]

Scott, F. D., "Sweden's Constructive Opposition to Emigration." *Journal of Modern History,* Vol. 37, 1965: 3. [Scott 1965.]

Semmingsen, Ingrid, *Veien mot Vest. Utvandringen fra Norge til Amerika, 1865–1915.* Vol. 2. (The Way West. Emigration from Norway to America.) Oslo 1950. [Semmingsen 1950.]

Simons, John, "Great Britain" in Berelson, B. (ed.), *Population Policy in Developed Countries.* New York 1974. [Simons 1974.]

Sjöstrand, Johannes, *Preliminär redogörelse för huvudresultaten av 1936 års partiella folkräkning, i vad denna avser barnantalet i bestående äktenskap ingångna efter år 1900.* (Preliminary report on main results of the 1936 census inasmuch as it concerned numbers of children in existing marriages entered after 1900.) Stockholm 1938. [Sjöstrand 1938.]

Sjöström, Kurt, *Socialpolitiken i det kapitalistiska samhället. Inledning till en marxistisk analys.* (Social policy in the captalist society. Introduction to a marxist analysis.) Göteborg 1974. [Sjöström 1974.]

Sjövall, H., "Äktenskapets hausse och baisse." (The rise and fall of marriage.) *Läkartidningen* 1970. [Sjövall 1970.]

Sociala meddelanden. (Social Bulletins.)

Socialutskottets betänkande 1977/78: 32. Befolkningsutvecklingen. (Report of the Parliamentary Social Committee, 1977/78: 32. Population development.)

Sommarin, Emil, *Befolkningsfrågan och jordbruket.* (The population question and agriculture.) Lund 1935. [Sommarin 1935.]

Spengler, J. J. – Duncan, O. D. (ed.), *Population Theory and Policy.* Glencoe 1956. [Spengler–Duncan 1956.]

Spengler, Joseph J., "Socioeconomic Theory and Population Policy" in Spengler, J. J. and Duncan, O. D., *Population Theory and Policy.* Glencoe 1956. [Spengler 1956.]

— *Population Change, Modernization, and Welfare.* Englewood Cliffs 1974. [Spengler 1974.]

Statens offentliga utredningar. 1935: 2. Betänkande med förslag rörande lån och årliga bidrag av statsmedel för främjande av bostadsförsörjning för mindre bemedlade barnrika familjer. (Swedish Government Official Reports. 1935: 2. Report with proposals on loans and annual grants from national funds for encouragement of the provision of housing for less well-to-do people with large families.) [*SOU* 1935: 2.]

— *1936: 14. Betänkande angående dels planmässigt sparande och dels statliga bosättningslån.* (Report on planned saving, and marriage loans.) [*SOU* 1936: 14.]

— *1936: 15. Betänkande angående moderskapspenning och mödrahjälp.* (Report on maternity bonus and maternity relief.) [*SOU* 1936: 15.]

— *1938: 57. Slutbetänkande avgivet av Befolkningskommissionen.* (Final report delivered by the Committee on Population.) [*SOU* 1938: 57.]

— *1943: 18. Utredning och förslag angående planmässigt sparande för familjebildning och statens bosättningslån.* (Inquiry and proposals on planned saving for family building, and marriage loans.) [*SOU* 1943: 18.]

— *1944: 26. Befolkningspolitik i utlandet. En redogörelse utarb. av 1941 års befolkningsutredning.* (Population policy abroad. Report prepared by the 1941 Population Commission.) [*SOU* 1944: 26.]

— *1945: 14. Socialpolitikens ekonomiska verkningar. Frågeställningar och riktlinjer. En undersökning av Carsten Welinder utförd på uppdrag av 1941 års befolkningskommission.* (Economic effects of social policy. Questions and approaches. An investigation by C. W. conducted at the request of the 1941 Population Commission.) [*SOU* 1945: 14.]

— *1945: 53. Statistiska undersökningar kring befolkningsfrågan utförda av 1941 års befolkningsutredning.* (Statistical investigations into the population question conducted by the 1941 Population Commission.) [*SOU* 1945: 53.]

149

— 1945: 63, 1947: 26. Bostadssociala utredningens slutbetänkande. (Final report of the Commission on Social Housing.) [SOU 1945: 63, 1947: 26.]

Statistisk årsbok för Sverige 1939. (Swedish annual statistics, 1939.) Stockholm 1939. [Statistisk årsbok 1939.]

Statistisk årsbok för Sverige 1940. (Swedish annual statistics 1940.) Stockholm 1940. [Statistisk årsbok 1940.]

Stefanow, Ivan – Naoumov, Nicola, "Bulgaria" in Berelson, B. (ed.), Population Policy in Developed Countries. New York 1974. [Stefanow–Naoumov 1974.]

Stockholms Adresskalender 1942. (Addresses in Stockholm. 1942.) Stockholm 1942.

Sundström, Kajsa, "Young People's Sexual Habits in Today's Swedish Society." Current Sweden, No. 125, 1976. [Sundström 1976.]

"Swedish Legislation on Birth Control—Contraception, Sterilization and Abortion" in Fact Sheets on Sweden. Published by the Swedish Institute. 1977.

Svenska stadsförbundets tidskrift 1943: 4. (Periodical of the Swedish Town Federation, 1943: 4.)

Svensk författningssamling. (Swedish Legislative Records.)

Svensson, Erik, "HSB:s och Hyresgäströrelsens samverkan—historia och framtid." (The cooperation between the National Association of the Tenants' Savings and Building Society and the Tenants' National Association—history and future perspective). In Samhället som det blev. Uppsatser om boende, bostadspolitik och bostadsproduktion. (Essays on housing, housing policies and housing production.) Stockholm 1976. [Svensson 1976.]

Sveriges Officiella Statistik 1936. (Sweden's Official Statistics.) "Allmänna bostadsräkningen år 1933." (General housing census.) [SOS 1936.]

— 1938. "Särskilda folkräkningen, 1935–36, III. (Extraordinary population census.) [SOS 1938.]

— "Befolkningsrörelsen. Översikt för åren 1951–60." (Population development. Survey for 1951–60.) Stockholm 1964. [SOS 1964.]

— "Folkmängden och dess förändringar, 1966." (Population size and its changes. 1966.) Stockholm 1967. [SOS 1967.]

Taeuber, Karl, "Cohort Migration." Demography 1966, 3: 2. [Taeuber 1966.]

Talmy, Robert, Histoire du mouvement familial en France, 1896–1939. Aubenas 1962. [Talmy 1962.]

Thomas, Dorothy S., Social and Economic Aspects of Swedish Population Movements 1750–1933. Stockholm Economic Studies 10: 2. New York 1941. [Thomas 1941.]

Torstendahl, Rolf, Mellan nykonservatism och liberalism. Idébrytningar inom högern och bondepartierna 1918–1934. (Between new-Conservatism and Liberalism. Conflicts within the Conservative and the Agrarian Parties, 1918–1934.) Studia Historica Upsaliensia 29. Uppsala 1969. [Torstendahl 1969.]

"Undersökning rörande mödrahjälpen under första halvåret 1939." (Investigation into maternity relief during the first six months of 1939) in Prop. 1940, urtima riksdagen: 5 bil. A. (In Government bills, extraordinary session of the riksdag.)

Utterström, G., Jordbrukets arbetare. Levnadsvillkor och arbetsliv på landsbygden från frihetstiden till mitten av 1800-talet. (Agricultural workers. Living conditions and working life from the Gustavian Era up to the mid-19th century.) 2 vols. Den svenska arbetarklassens historia, 13. (History of the Swedish working class.) Stockholm 1957. [Utterström 1957.]

— "Labour Policy and Population Thought in Eighteenth Century Sweden." SEHR, vol. X, 2: 1962. [Utterström 1962.]

Vadakin, James C., *Family Allowances. An Analysis of Their Development and Implications.* Miami 1958. [Vadakin 1958.]

Valentei, Dmitri J., "Soviet Union" in Berelson, B. (ed.), *Population Policy in Developed Countries.* New York 1974. [Valentei 1974.]

Veevers, Jean, "Voluntary Childlessness: A Review of Issues and Evidence." *Marriage and Family Review* 1979. [Veevers 1979.]

Wicksell, K., *Några ord om samhällsolyckornas viktigaste orsak och botemedel med särskilt avseende på dryckenskapen. Med ett bihang.* (Some words on the cause and cure of the most important reason behind social degeneration, with particular regard to inebriation.) Uppsala 1880. [Wicksell 1880.]

— "Uttalande i emigrationsfrågan." (Statement on the emigration question.) In *Emigrationsutredningen, XVIII.* Uttalanden i emigrationsfrågan af Svenska vetenskapsmän afgifna på begäran af Emigrationsutredningen. (Statements on the emigration question by Swedish scientists prepared at the request of the Emigration Committee.) Stockholm 1910. [Wicksell 1910.]

Wicksell, Sven D., "PM angående äktenskapsbildningen i Sverige." (PM concerning marriage in Sweden.) *SOU* 1936: 14. [S. Wicksell 1936.]

Wicksell, S. D. – Quensel, C.-E., "Undersökning av de demografiska elementen i deras regionala variationer och sammanhang." (Investigation of demographic elements in their regional variation and situation.) *SOU* 1938: 24. [Wicksell–Quensel 1938.]

Willcox, W. F., (ed.), *International Migrations.* Vols. I, II. New York 1929, 1931. [Willcox 1931.]

Wilson, Elizabeth, *Women and the Welfare State.* London 1977. [Wilson 1977.]

Winberg, C., *Folkökning och proletarisering. Kring den sociala strukturomvandlingen på Sveriges landsbygd under den agrara revolutionen.* Meddelanden från Historiska institutionen i Göteborg, 10. (Population growth and proletarianisation. The transformation of social structures in rural Sweden during the agrarian revolution. Report from the Dept. of History, Univ. of Gothenburg, 10.) Partille 1975. [Winberg 1975.]

Wolfe, A. B., "The Population Problem Since the World War: A Survey of Literature and Research" in Spengler, J. J. and Duncan, O. D. (eds.), *Population Theory and Policy.* 1928, repr. Glencoe 1956. [Wolfe 1956.]

de Voursney, Mair J., "Theory and Method in Population Policy Research" in Clinton, Richard L. (ed.), *Population and Politics. New Directions in Political Science Research.* Toronto–London 1973. [de Voursney 1973.]

Ziolkowski, Janusz A., "Poland" in Berelson, B. (ed.), *Population Policy in Developed Countries.* New York 1974. [Ziolkowski 1974.]

Åkerlund, Erik, "Befolkningsfrågan och ärftlighetsläran. En rasbiologisk granskning av den Myrdalska framställningen." *Stockholms-Tidningen* 25.4.1935. (The population question and heredity. A social biology investigation of the proposal by the Myrdals.) [Åkerlund 1935.]

Östling, Gösta (ed.), *Borås.* (Svenska stadsmonografier.) Borås 1949. (Borås. In Monographs of Swedish towns.) [Östling 1949.]

151

Selective Index

Acta Universitatis Upsaliensis
STUDIA HISTORICA UPSALIENSIA

Editories: Sven A. Nilsson, Sten Carlsson, Carl Göran Andræ

1. *Gustaf Jonasson:* Karl XII och hans rådgivare. Den utrikespolitiska maktkampen i Sverige 1697–1702. 1960.
2. *Sven Lundkvist:* Gustav Vasa och Europa. Svensk handels- och utrikespolitik 1534–1557. 1960.
3. *Tage Linder:* Biskop Olof Wallquists politiska verksamhet till och med riksdagen 1789. 1960.
4. *Carl Göran Andræ:* Kyrka och frälse i Sverige under äldre medeltid. 1960.
5. *Bengt Henningsson:* Geijer som historiker. 1961.
6. *Nils Runeby:* Monarchia mixta. Maktfördelningsdebatt i Sverige under stormaktstiden. 1962.
7. *Åke Hermansson:* Karl IX och ständerna. Tronfrågan och författningsutvecklingen 1598–1611. 1962.
8. Hundra års historisk diskussion. Historiska föreningen i Uppsala 1862–1962. 1962.
9. *Sten Carlsson:* Byråkrati och borgarstånd under frihetstiden. 1963.
10. *Gunnar Christie Wasberg:* Forsvarstanke og suverenitetsprinsipp. Kretsen om Aftonposten i den unionspolitiske debatt 1890–mars 1905. 1963.
11. *Kurt Ågren:* Adelns bönder och kronans. Skatter och besvär i Uppland 1650–1680. 1964.
12. *Michael Nordberg:* Les ducs et la royauté. Etudes sur la rivalité des ducs d'Orléans et de Bourgogne 1392–1407. 1964.
13. *Stig Hadenius:* Fosterländsk unionspolitik. Majoritetspartiet, regeringen och unionsfrågan 1888–1899. 1964.
14. *Stellan Dahlgren:* Karl X Gustav och reduktionen. 1964.
15. *Rolf Torstendahl:* Källkritik och vetenskapssyn i svensk historisk forskning 1820–1920. 1964.
16. *Stefan Björklund:* Oppositionen vid 1823 års riksdag. Jordbrukskris och borgerlig liberalism. 1964.
17. *Håkan Berggren & Göran B. Nilsson:* Liberal spcialpolitik 1853–1884. Två studier. 1965.
18. *Torsten Burgman:* Svensk opinion och diplomati under rysk-japanska kriget 1904–1905. 1965.
19. *Eric Wärenstam:* Sveriges Nationella Ungdomsförbund och högern 1928–1934. 1965.
20. *Torgny Nevéus:* Ett betryggande försvar.

Värnplikten och arméorganisationen i svensk politik 1880–1885. 1965.
21. *Staffan Runestam:* Förstakammarhögern och rösträttsfrågan 1900–1907. 1966.
22. *Stig Ekman:* Slutstriden om representationsreformen. 1966.
23. *Gunnar Herrström:* 1927 års skolreform. En studie i svensk skolpolitik 1918–1927. 1966.
24. *Sune Åkerman:* Skattereformen 1810. Ett experiment med progressiv inkomstskatt. 1967.
25. *Göran B. Nilsson:* Självstyrelsens problematik. Undersökningar i svensk landstingshistoria 1839–1928. 1967.
26. *Klaus-Richard Böhme:* Bremisch-verdische Statsfinanzen 1645–1676. Die schwedische Krone als deutsche Landesherrin. 1967.
27. *Gustaf Jonasson:* Karl XII:s polska politik 1702–1703. 1968.
28. *Hans Landberg:* Statsfinans och kungamakt. Karl X Gustav inför polska kriget. 1969.
29. *Rolf Torstendahl:* Mellan nykonservatism och liberalism. Idébrytningar inom högern och bondepartierna 1918–1934. 1969.
30. *Nils Runeby:* Den nya världen och den gamla. Amerikabild och emigrationsuppfattning i Sverige 1820–1860. 1969.
31. *Fred Nilsson:* Emigrationen från Stockholm till Nordamerika 1880–1893. En studie i urban utvandring. 1970.
32. *Curt Johansson:* Lantarbetarna i Uppland 1918–1930. En studie i facklig taktik och organisation. 1970.
33. *Arndt Öberg:* De yngre mössorna och deras utländska bundsförvanter 1765–1769. Med särskild hänsyn till de kommersiella och politiska förbindelserna med Storbritannien, Danmark och Preussen. 1970.
34. *Torgny Börjeson:* Metall 20 – fackföreningen och människan. 1971.
35. *Harald Runblom:* Svenska företag i Latinamerika. Etableringsmönster och förhandlingstaktik 1900–1940. 1971.
36. *Hans Landberg, Lars Ekholm, Roland Nordlund & Sven A. Nilsson:* Det kontinentala krigets ekonomi. Studier i krigsfinansiering under svensk stormaktstid. 1971.
37. *Sture Lindmark:* Swedish America 1914–1932. Studies in Ethnicity with Emphasis on Illinois and Minnesota. 1971.

38. *Ulf Beijbom:* Swedes in Chicago. A Demographic and Social Study of the 1846–1880 Immigration. 1971.

39. *Staffan Smedberg:* Frälsebonderörelser i Halland och Skåne 1772–76. 1972.

40. *Björn Rondahl:* Emigration, folkomflyttning och säsongarbete i ett sågverksdistrikt i södra Hälsingland 1865–1910. Söderala kommun med särskild hänsyn till Ljusne industrisamhälle. 1972.

41. *Ann-Sofie Kälvemark:* Reaktionen mot utvandringen. Emigrationsfrågan i svensk debatt och politik 1901–1904. 1972.

42. *Lars-Göran Tedebrand:* Västernorrland och Nordamerika 1875–1913. Utvandring och återinvandring. 1972.

43. *Ann-Marie Petersson:* Nyköping under frihetstiden. Borgare och byråkrater i den lokala politiken. 1972. (Ej i bokhandeln)

44. *Göran Andolf:* Historien på gymnasiet. Undervisning och läroböcker 1820–1965. 1972.

45. *Jan Sundin:* Främmande studenter vid Uppsala universitet före andra världskriget. En studie i studentmigration. 1973.

46. *Christer Öhman:* Nyköping och hertigdömet 1568–1622. 1973. (Ej i bokhandeln)

47. *Sune Åkerman, Ingrid Eriksson, David Gaunt, Anders Norberg, John Rogers & Kurt Ågren:* Aristocrats, farmers and proletarians. Essays in Swedish Demographic History. 1973.

48. *Uno Westerlund:* Borgarsamhällets upplösning och självstyrelsens utveckling i Nyköping 1810–1880. (Ej i bokhandeln)

49. *Sven Hedenskog:* Folkrörelserna i Nyköping 1880–1915. Uppkomst, social struktur och politisk aktivitet. 1973. (Ej i bokhandeln)

50. *Berit Brattne:* Bröderna Larsson. En studie i svensk emigrantagentverksamhet under 1880-talet. 1973.

51. *Anders Kullberg:* Johan Gabriel Stenbock och reduktionen. Godspolitik och ekonomiförvaltning 1675–1705. 1973.

52. *Gunilla Ingmar:* Monopol på nyheter. Ekonomiska och politiska aspekter på svenska och internationella nyhetsbyråers verksamhet 1870–1919. 1973.

53. *Sven Lundkvist:* Politik, nykterhet och reformer. En studie i folkrörelsernas politiska verksamhet 1900–1920. 1974.

54. *Kari Tarkiainen:* "Vår gamble Arffiende Ryssen". Synen på Ryssland i Sverige 1595–1621 och andra studier kring den svenska Rysslandsbilden från tidigare stormaktstid. 1974.

55. *Bo Öhngren:* Folk i rörelse. Samhällsutveckling, flyttningsmönster och folkrörelser i Eskilstuna 1870–1900. 1974.

56. *Lars Ekholm:* Svensk krigsfinansiering 1630–1631. 1974.

57. *Roland Nordlund:* Krig på avveckling. Sverige och tyska kriget 1633. 1974.

58. *Clara Nevéus:* Trälarna i landskapslagarnas samhälle. Danmark och Sverige. 1974.

59. *Bertil Johansson:* Social differentiering och kommunalpolitik. Enköping 1863–1919. 1974.

60. *Jan Lindroth:* Idrottens väg till folkrörelse. Studier i svensk idrottsrörelse till 1915. 1974.

61. *Richard B. Lucas:* Charles August Lindbergh, Sr.–A Case Study of Congressional Insurgency, 1906–1912. 1974.

62. *Hans Norman:* Från Bergslagen till Nordamerika. Studier i migrationsmönster, social rörlighet och demografisk struktur med utgångspunkt från Örebro län 1851–1915. 1974.

63. *David Gaunt:* Utbildning till statens tjänst. En kollektivbiografi av stormaktstidens hovrättsauskultanter. 1975.

64. *Eibert Ernby:* Adeln och bondejorden. En studie rörande skattefrälset i Oppunda härad under 1600-talet. 1975.

65. *Bo Kronborg & Thomas Nilsson:* Stadsflyttare. Industrialisering, migration och social mobilitet med utgångspunkt från Halmstad, 1870–1910. 1975.

66. *Rolf Torstendahl:* Teknologins nytta. Motiveringar för det svenska tekniska utbildningsväsendet framväxt framförda av riksdagsmän och utbildningsadministratörer 1810–1870. 1975.

67. *Allan Ranehök:* Centralmakt och domsmakt. Studier kring den högsta rättskipningen i kung Magnus Erikssons länder 1319–1355. 1975.

68. *James Cavallie:* Från fred till krig. De finansiella problemen kring krigsutbrottet år 1700. 1975.

69. *Ingrid Åberg:* Förening och politik. Folkrörelsernas politiska aktivitet i Gävle under 1800-talet. 1975.

70. *Margareta Revera:* Gods och gård 1650–1680. Magnus Gabriel De la Gardies godsbildning och godsdrift i Västergötland. I. 1975.

71. *Aleksander Loit:* Kampen om feodalräntan. Reduktionen och domänpolitiken i Estland 1655–1710. 1975.

72. *Torgny Lindgren:* Banko- och riksgäldsrevisionerna 1782–1807. "De redliga män, som bevakade ständers rätt." 1975.

73. *Rolf Torstendahl:* Dispersion of Engineers in a Transitional Society. Swedish Technicians 1860–1940. 1975.

74. From Sweden to America. A History of the Migration. Red. Harald Runblom & Hans Norman. 1976.

75. *Svante Jakobsson:* Från fädernejord till förfäders land. 1976.
76. *Lars Åkerblom:* Sir Samuel Hoare och Etiopienkonflikten 1935. 1976.
77. *Gustaf Jonasson:* Per Edvin Sköld 1946–1951. 1976.
78. *Sören Winge:* Die Wirtschaftliche Aufbau-Vereinigung (WAV) 1945–53. Entwicklung und Politik einer „undoktrinären" politischen Partei in der Bundesrepublik in der ersten Nachkriegszeit. 1976.
79. *Klaus Misgeld:* Die "Internationale Gruppe demokratischer sozialisten" in Stockholm 1942–1945. Zur sozialistischen Friedensdiskussion während des Zweiten Weltkrieges. 1976.
80. *Roland Karlman:* Evidencing Historical Classifications in British and American Historiography 1930–1970. 1976.
81. *Berndt Fredriksson:* Försvarets finansiering. Svensk krigsekonomi under skånska kriget 1675–79. 1976.
82. *Karl Englund:* Arbetarförsäkringsfrågan i svensk politik 1884–1901. 1976.
83. *Nils Runeby.* Teknikerna, vetenskapen och kulturen. Ingenjörsundervisning och ingenjörsorganisationer i 1870-talets Sverige. 1976.
84. *Erland F. Josephson:* SKP och Komintern 1921–1924. Motsättningarna inom Sveriges Kommunistiska Parti och dess relationer till den Kommunistiska Internationalen. 1976.
85. *Sven Lundkvist:* Folkrörelserna i det svenska samhället 1850–1920. 1976.
86. *Bo Öhngren:* GEOKOD. En kodlista för den administrativa indelningen i Sverige 1862–1951. 1977.
87. *Mike L. Samson:* Population Mobility in the Netherlands 1880–1910. A Case Study of Wisch in the Achterhoek. 1977.
88. *Ugbana Okpu:* Ethnic Minority Problems in Nigerian Politics: 1960–1965, 1977.
89. *Gunnar Carlsson:* Enköping under frihetstiden. Social struktur och lokal politik. 1977.
90. *Sten Carlsson:* Fröknar, mamseller, jungfrur och pigor. Ogifta kvinnor i det svenska ståndssamhället. 1977.
91. *Rolf Pålbrant:* Arbetarrörelsen och idrotten 1919–1939. 1977.
92. *Viveca Halldin Norberg:* Swedes in Haile Selassie's Ethiopia 1924–1952. A Study in Early Development Co-operation. 1977.
93. *Holger Wester:* Innovationer i befolkningsrörligheten. En studie av spridningsförlopp i befolkningsrörligheten utgående från Petalax socken i Österbotten. 1977.
94. *Jan Larsson:* Diplomati och industriellt genombrott. Svenska exportsträvanden på Kina 1906–1916. 1977.

95. *Rolf Nygren:* Disciplin, kritikrätt och rättssäkerhet. Studier kring militieombudsmannaämbetets (MO) doktrin- och tillkomsthistoria 1901–1915. 1977.
96. *Kenneth Awebro:* Gustav III:s räfst med ämbetsmännen 1772–1799 – aktionerna mot landshövdingarna och Göta hovrätt. 1977.
97. *Eric De Geer:* Migration och influensfält. Studier av emigration och intern migration i Finland och Sverige 1816–1972. 1977.
98. *Sigbrit Plaenge Jacobson:* 1766-års allmänna fiskestadga. Dess uppkomst och innebörd med hänsyn till Bottenhavsfiskets rättsfrågor. 1978.
99. *Ingvar Flink:* Strejkbryteriet och arbetets frihet. En studie av svensk arbetsmarknad fram till 1938. 1978.
100. *Ingrid Eriksson & John Rogers:* Rural Labor and Population Change. Social and Demographic Developments in East-Central Sweden during the Nineteenth Century. 1978.
101. *Kerstin Moberg:* Från tjänstehjon till hembiträde. En kvinnlig låglönegrupp i den fackliga kampen 1903–1946. 1978.
102. *Mezri Bdira:* Relations internationales et sousdéveloppement. La Tunisie 1857–1864. 1978.
103. *Ingrid Hammarström, Väinö Helgesson, Barbro Hedvall, Christer Knuthammar & Bodil Wallin:* Ideologi och socialpolitik i 1800-talets Sverige. 4 studier. 1978.
104. *Gunnar Sundberg:* Partipolitik och regionala intressen 1755–1766. Studier kring det bottniska handelstvångets hävande. 1978.
105. *Kekke Stadin:* Småstäder, småborgare och stora samhällsförändringar. Borgarnas sociala struktur i Arboga, Enköping och Västervik under perioden efter 1680. 1979.
106. *Åke Lindström:* Bruksarbetarfackföreningar. Metalls avdelningar vid bruken i östra Västmanlands län före 1911. 1979.
107. *Mats Rolén:* Skogsbygd i omvandling. Studier kring befolkningsutveckling, omflyttning och social rörlighet i Revsunds tingslag 1829–1977. 1979.
108. *János Perényi:* Revolutionsuppfattningens anatomi. 1848 års revolutioner i svensk debatt. 1979.
109. *Kent Sivesand:* Skifte och befolkning. Skiftenas inverkan på byar och befolkning i Mälarregionen. 1979.
110. *Thomas Lindkvist:* Landborna i Norden under äldre medeltid. 1979.
111. *Björn M. Edsman:* Lawyers in Gold Coast Politics c. 1900–1945. From Mensah Sarbah to J. B. Danquah. 1979.

112. *Svante Jakobsson:* Osilia–Maritima 1227–1346. Studier kring tillkomsten av svenska bosättningar i Balticum, i synnerhet inom biskopsstiftet Ösel-Wiek. 1980.
113. *Jan Stattin:* Hushållningssällskapen och agrarsamhällets förändring-utveckling och verksamhet under 1800-talets första hälft. 1980.
114. *Bertil Lundvik:* Solidaritet och partitaktik. Den svenska arbetarrörelsen och spanska inbördeskriget 1936–1939. 1980.
115. *Ann-Sofie Kälvemark:* More Children of Better Quality? Aspects on Swedish Population Policy in the 1930's. 1980.